MAMAPHONIC

MAMAPHONIC

*Balancing
Motherhood
and
Other
Creative
Acts*

EDITED BY

BEE LAVENDER

and MAIA ROSSINI

Mamaphonic: 1-932360-64-6

Front cover: Stella Mars
Back cover & book design: Gary Fogelson

Published by Soft Skull Press
71 Bond Street, Brooklyn, NY 11217

Distributed by Publishers Group West
www.pgw.com | 1.800.788.3123

Printed in Canada

CONTENTS

MAMAPHONIC

INTRODUCTION

BEE LAVENDER & MAIA ROSSINI

THE STORY of editing this book is a story that all mothers who are artists already know by heart. It is a story about hiding out in a room while a child calls out for assistance, answering back, *Just one more minute!* while we try to finish reading another essay. It is a story of starts and stops, of catching time, forcing time, making time whenever we could get it. Sitting in a car, waiting for school to let out, frantically scribbling something on the back of an envelope before the kids descend. Compromise, planning, and hard work.

We know this story, we live this story, we sit over tea and coffee, watching our children and worrying this story, shaking it out, smoothing it down, telling it over and over with all the other mothers we know.

How do you do it? we ask each other. Do you think we'll ever do it again? Is it worth it? Is it possible? Is it better? Is it worse? Will we ever have the time, the brains, the skill, the will to do it the way it should be done?

We collect other mothers in our heads—mothers who have published books, mothers who have opened shows, mothers who sell their art, mothers who act in movies, mothers who sell millions of records, mothers who go on the road.

We repeat their names like prayer: Toni Morrison, Louise Erdrich, Exene Cervenka, Kim Gordon, Sinead O'Connor, Diane di Prima, George Sand, Kristen Hersh, Erma Bombeck, Mary Wollstonecraft, Patti Smith, Tillie Olsen, Grace Paley, Ursula Le Guin,

Muriel Rukesyer, Diane Arbus, Lorrie Moore, Louise Nevelson, Sally Mann, Maya Angelou, Loretta Lynn.

We think of Shirley Jackson writing "The Lottery" in her head as she pushed a pram to the market. We think of Jean Kerr editing "Please Don't Eat the Daisies" in her office, a car parked one block from the family home. We think of Betty MacDonald dreaming up her next cheerful bestseller (the source of her family's income) from her bed in a tuberculosis asylum. We look for examples from history of women who did not have our advantages growing up after the massive educational and cultural reforms rendered by second wave feminism.

We see ourselves in the words of Angela Carter when she writes, "There are lots of things that you can brush under the carpet about yourself until you're faced with somebody whose needs won't be put off."

We are respectfully amazed by the example of the Carter Family transmitting a musical legacy across generations of strong women. We scan magazines looking for contemporary examples of powerful, successful female artists and find Yoko Ono, who lost one child in a custody dispute and then raised another on her own after her husband was murdered. She says, "Work is something I love, and is what comes naturally to me. Business is harder. Motherhood is extremely complicated and difficult, though I suppose some mothers would say it's as natural as breathing."

We worry about the fact that many of our role models succumbed to addiction, mental illness, and suicide. We laugh out loud when we hear the refrain of a Freakwater song that goes, "It's not hard to have a little baby / And I won't have far to go when I go crazy."

We hold these examples in our minds when our own lives get too slippery, when we have no space or time to pursue our work separate from the demands of our children.

Somehow they did it, we think. So we can do it too.

This book is a response to the question *How do they do it?* This book started from a practical place, in conversations with other women. The women we know want inspiration but they have pragmatic concerns: how to find a good printer, where to find a grad program with decent daycare, how to navigate agents and find gallery representation, how to keep the kids out of expensive art supplies, how to negotiate time with their parenting partners, or, often, how to negotiate time when there is no parenting partner.

The women we know proudly talk about involving their children in their art and are not afraid to say that sometimes they need absolute solitude as well. These women insist on a room of their own, even if it's simply a bedroom with a door that shuts or a space created out of hung blankets, a cushion on the floor, and a serious demand for an hour or two to themselves.

The women we know have a palpable need for community. They know the theory, they practice the work. They need something else—examples from history, peers in their chosen fields, the kinds of resources and networks that come with belonging to a guild or benevolent society.

This book starts with the premise that people require practical models. We acknowledge that women's work often happens outside of accepted history. We do not accept the lie that having children kills creativity. In fact, we assert that people who are raising kids have to be more creative to find enough time to do their work, to figure out

3

ways to integrate their children into their art, to strike that balance between the needs of their families and the requirements of their work.

When we decided to do this book we knew there would be a strong response. We knew that the topic of balancing motherhood with an artistic career was one that women had a lot to talk about. But even with those kinds of expectations, we were over-whelmed by the response. With a very limited call for submissions, mainly based on for-warded e-mail and word of mouth, we received over four hundred submissions.

The idea for this anthology started on the road, when Bee did readings around the country. Countless women asked, "How do you do it?" and seemed to need more than just the brief and idiosyncratic account of one mother. They needed examples from all sorts of mothers and artists. When Maia did a reading at her local bookstore, this proj-ect was briefly mentioned in her introduction. After the reading, she was surrounded by a knot of women and none of them had anything to say about her story. They wanted to know about *Mamaphonic*. They asked, *When is it coming out? Are you still taking sub-missions? I'm so glad someone is finally putting something like this together!*

This book tells the truth about the way we live, the words we have said. Every sin-gle essay made us nod in agreement; every single essay told an important story of women who actively and consciously choose to be both mothers and artists. There were compromises of vision, of time, of careers. There were missed opportunities, grief, per-severance, transcendence, and pleasure.

In the end we selected the stories that covered as many different aspects of the experience as possible. We have poets and novelists and a flamenco dancer. We have singers and painters and a film critic. We have comic book illustrators, zine publishers, a photographer, and a baker. We have scholars and playwrights and rock stars.

This is a book we hope women will feel compelled to share with friends. We hope they will pass it on saying, *You need to read this. This will help.*

We hope that new mothers will read stories like Ingrid Wendt's and Lisa Peet's, women who have been balancing their work and their children for years, and see that things happen in cycles, that they will get through those intense early years and have time to work again. We hope that mothers whose children have already grown up and left their houses will read work like J. Anderson Coat's and Rachel Hall's and have those early years reawakened in their memories, that they will think about what they learned. Ayun Halliday and Jen Thorpe remind us that there is no reason we can't change the rules and make both creative work and a creatively organized career. In fact, we are entitled— we are, after all, mothers.

Our own children informed each page of this book. They were constantly present during the process, asking for a glass of water, for help getting their shirt buttoned, for a ride, to go to a movie. They leaned against our shoulders demanding that it was their turn at the computer, asking, *Mom, aren't you done yet? When can we play?* There is no doubt that they made this process longer and harder than it might have been otherwise. But without them this book simply wouldn't exist. And surely all of our contributors would agree with that particular sentiment. Artists are by no means ordinary people, and artists with children often face extraordinary pressures to conform or to change. This gig isn't easy.

Motherhood might slow down art. Children might interrupt those moments of concentration. We're not saying that this is the easiest path to take, but we flatly refuse to agree with the idea that becoming a mother is the end because it is not. It is the beginning.

NOODLES AND SAUCE

INGRID WENDT

No one sees a flower, not really.
To look at a flower takes time, like having a friend.
— *Georgia O'Keefe*

NORA, young poet, wife, young mother, you write of despair. You're turning, you say, into "a mom from hell." Your three year-old needs constant social interaction. He never leaves your side, he's cautious "beyond belief," speaks in a nearly inaudible tone, "freaks out" when you misunderstand him (which is every twenty minutes or so). "The actual temper tantrum isn't so bad," you say, "it's the anticipation. If a lover or husband or friend treated you this way you would *never* speak to that person again."

On the other hand your younger one, eighteen months, is so independent he needs constant watching so he won't hurt himself or anyone else. He runs and climbs and tries to force affection on other kids on the playground who "don't like this so much." Two days ago you took him to the emergency room for stitches in his face. You don't, you say, have "the personality or staying power for this kind of vigilant motherhood, not to mention how impossible it is with my other kid around."

And you have assistance: three days of day care, a participatory husband and grandparents, sometimes babysitters. It's not that you don't get time to yourself. What, you wonder, could be wrong with you? "Lately, it's just misery. . . . Sometimes I'm not sure . . .

poetry or anything even really exists or that I will ever be able to look at noodles and sauce without feeling a desperate, bitter anger."

Nora, what can I say that will help? I try to respond. I send you a poem of my own, written almost thirty years back with a wry humor crafted to disguise the actual depths of it. Here, with a title borrowed from poet Dylan Thomas ("Portrait of the Artist as a Young Dog"), borrowed from novelist James Joyce (*Portrait of the Artist as a Young Man*), from my first book of poems:

PORTRAIT OF THE POET AS A YOUNG BITCH

A nice girl like her in this mess.
Always in debt she's writing from hand to mouth
stealing moments for lines like bread
from her husband, daughter, herself. Whole days
she isn't there at all.

Days when she is she pays for it
with sleep. The interest piles up
over her head, poems like dreams
alarm clocks won't let her remember.

These things she discovers women before
her knew and never were able to
name, their needs sticking out
like porcupine quills, no one
could get close enough to help.

These images filling her mind like the house
she'll never catch up on, the indecent
places they appear: dishwater,
tubs full of diapers, sheets
slick with sperm.

When they don't wash out she
stuffs them in the pantry like nuts.
By summer their edges have molded.
Nothing ever fits.

These things she would like to believe
are good and hasn't heard anyone say: over
due periods she'll worry
out like a loose tooth: outlines
of lives like hers she hasn't seen
herself in until now. One hand between

her breasts, the other
between her teeth, she'll write
to make an honest woman of herself.

Looking back, reading these words, the feelings all come back: how I felt so alone in this new motherhood, unprepared and without the resources to cope. All I could do, at the time, was try to name what was going on: to put the experience into words, to find metaphors for it—which is, after all, what we poets do, right? What you are doing too, even now, in your words about your sons.

Other poets answer your SOS (which you've posted on the women poets listserv to which we subscribe) with anecdotes, memories, more poems. "Been there, survived that." You're normal, we tell you; we know how it is to feel so fragmented, so at the beck and call of the needs of children. We know how impossible it is to feel oneself a writer when one is hardly a "self" anymore; when physical tasks and sleep deprivation and the need to be always available all conspire to rob young mothers of the ability to carry thoughts to their conclusions, or even (I remember it well) to finish a simple, spoken sentence, to keep in mind, one second to next, where a thought was headed. If I didn't even have time to pick flowers, how could I ever hope to write poems again?

We offer suggestions. Rachel Barenblat suggests reading Anne Lamott's Operating Instructions, a journal of her first year of single-motherhood. Helen Frost counsels on the importance of letting go of the natural desire to change your children's behavior, and let yourself have more fun with them, join them, when you can't be writing, in their play. We tell you to "hang in there, this too shall pass" and "far too quickly," we say, "you'll see!"

How far we've come, Nora, we women writers, from the vast silence that surrounded us, in our own days of young motherhood! What comfort I found then in reading two key texts: Tillie Olsen's "Silences," in which I learned that "writer's block" is far more common (especially for women) than I'd ever supposed, and survivable; and Virginia Woolf's *A Room of One's Own*, in which I first became conscious of (and suddenly understood) the fact that the vast majority of women writers, up to our present time, had been single, or childless, or both.

And yet, and yet. . . . There is the comfort of knowing one is not alone, there is the comfort of looking forward to the end of fragmentation (though that is something of a myth, in my mind—our attention is always and forever altered and tuned to our children's needs and realities, along with or sometimes even ahead of our own, even when they're grown). Is there nothing to do but endure? Is there not also something we can change, something to actively *do*, to take from these moments of being more mother than writer that will let us return (when time and circumstances permit) as better poets than before?

I think there is. But it's hard to describe. I don't have a poem for it. I do know that to take charge of the present, to stay alive as a writer, involves learning not just to gracefully abandon the hours we used to give to our writing, but also to let go of other expectations and fears, bred from what we've been led to believe poets should do.

"If we are poets, real poets, we write every day, no matter what." Right? Wrong. I've gone days, even months without writing anything or feeling like writing anything, each time fearing I'm forever washed up as a writer, that I'm never going to write again, and finding each time, that I can return to my work (when impulse and circumstance are aligned) as one returns to a true friendship after long absence and picks up where we left off. What a surprise it always has been, and the memory of that surprise has made it easier, each time, to trust it will happen again. It rekindles my will to keep seeking out that precious hour or two or three when, like Georgia O'Keefe looking at flowers, I know my vision will return.

Another false dictate: poets with no free time during the day should get up each morning, before the rest of the house is awake, right? (But what if our bodies and minds do not work that way?) And another: writing skills, unused, wither and die. Maybe for some, but, dear Nora, that's not my experience. Somehow, magically, each time I've been kept from my work I find my writing skills have kept pace with my understanding—my sense of craft has actually grown—assuming I've been thinking and reading and paying attention to where I am and what I've been doing each day.

And maybe that's part of the key, paying attention. My sister gave me a book for my birthday titled *Wherever You Go, There You Are*, by Jon Kabat-Zinn, a book about "mindfulness." Reading it, I see there are ways of being "fully present" I have yet to learn. But if I've learned one thing it's that regret at being in one place and not another is never going to let me enjoy where I am or get enough out of today to enrich tomorrow.

"Write only if you must," instructed Rilke, in one of his letters to a young poet. This used to worry me: if some days I didn't feel I must write, I must not be a true writer! Today, I see it afresh: if some days I don't feel like writing, and am aware of that fact, I am, because I'm a writer, not only experiencing that fact, I'm living other things and being aware of them too, and hopefully learning something. Who knows what? It's too soon to ask. What if Rilke meant "Write it down only if you can find a way, but never doubt you are growing as a writer."

One of the conditions of being a writer—and this is something you already know—is that we don't just see things, we see ourselves seeing. We don't just have a thought, we know we are having it. Words flit through our minds, observations, and the poet in us goes, "Aha! Good line!" or "Hey, good image!" Not always, not every moment, but often enough for us to be aware that we aren't simply like everyone else who thinks and therefore is. Do we stop doing this just because we aren't writing? Does this ability (akin to a compulsion) dry up and go away? Or is it something we can't help doing, and can learn to cultivate and utilize?

One piece of helpful advice that keeps getting passed among writers and teachers of writing originated with my own beloved teacher, a poet named William Stafford, friend and mentor to many poets of my generation and beyond. When asked what he did when he got writer's block, Bill replied, "I lower my standards." Which doesn't mean, of course, he didn't revise or raise the quality of his poems between rough draft stage to published piece.

What if, dear Nora and other young poets reading this today, we didn't expect a finished poem each day, each week, or even each time we sat down to write? What if we did-

9

n't sit down—as we've often been told to do, and have maybe told others —with one line and follow that thread to see where it leads? Sometimes that works, true. But we can't force it. You know that already. And when it doesn't, what if we could just lower our standards enough to write down, every now and then, that one good line flitting through our consciousness before it floats out of reach: that dandelion puff, that milkweed feather like those I learned, as a child, to catch and make a wish on and release? What if your comment about noodles and sauce could be turned into metaphor, tucked away somewhere on paper or in your mind, could become food for a poem? (I tucked it away in my own mind, as you see.) And, as Helen has pointed out, your words show you are being a writer in your message to us, even as you despair.

What if we could be more deliberate in our collection of these little language scraps, these spices, these pieces of fabric, and when we had a moment or two away from the kids, or the bills, or the job, we could sort through and cluster and group them, just as a quilter puts together matching pieces of cloth, or a cook, the saved ingredients? It's not something we often hear about, this way of writing, though I've little doubt there are other writers who've learned, like me, to write by doing piecework, who've learned to trust the unconscious mind to have a logic all its own. Writer's who've found that after days or weeks or longer of collecting words, lines, images, we can see patterns emerging: themes, subjects, recurring thoughts, new angles on old ideas. They add up to something. For me, for us, writing as "an act of discovery" is the process of discovering that sum.

Here's another, more recent—yet oddly incomplete—poem of my own, written perhaps ten years ago, revised many times. I may still be working on it. It's a kind of confession, an admission of still being vulnerable to another kind of block that plagues more of us, I suspect, than admit it. For even when the demands of children and aging parents and spouses and past good intentions are absent for even a short while, there's that deep-seated need we sometimes have to know the whole story, to make sense of it before we can write. How often we were advised, as students, to know what we were going to say before we said it!

THE SIMPLE TRUTH
Write only if you must. —Rainer Maria Rilke

Not often, this luxury: hours of writing time
Blessedly stretching, bright tail of a comet over my desk,
This invitation to hop aboard and ride, look down at my words
From some stratospheric perspective: time to say
What I see and be clear. Still,

Some days I'll do almost anything else,
Wander the house, tackle the ironing, dusting, I'll shuffle
This pile of papers, those books, to another more sensible place,
As though the hand could fix what they eye cannot, a way to tend to
All sides of each case—as if waiting,

10

That underground river, might lead to One Word joining
All versions, all multiple impulses, all known ways of
Perceiving. And what do I get? Tributaries
Silting the honest depths of Feeling.

One of my therapist friends no doubt has a name for this.
Yesterday, speaking of clients, she used the word *Closure*,
Meaning what you aim for
When something is still unresolved.

How I envy her strict vocabulary.
Words like signposts, lighthouses. With them
Some people know where they are and go on.

How I would like to call myself *Constant. Faithful.*
To know if this obsession, or really the simple truth knocking
To get back into the world:

One shining leap out of water that doesn't fall back,
One trail of a shooting star visible clear to the end.

How, like a child spelling the secret of sparklers,
Letter by letter, I

Would write all of its bright, golden name in the air.

Do you hear me, Nora, writing to myself at this point as much as to you? I've had this essay in mind for several weeks, didn't know where it was going (oh, that familiar block) and so kept taking notes, many of which I haven't used, kept wandering around the house, tending to others, to everyday concerns. (Yes, it still happens.) Today, the pieces are taking shape, a line I wasn't expecting to use, the line from your message, "noodles and sauce," suddenly floated through my head, it seemed the ideal title and I caught it. I looked again at your post. Your line "a mom from hell," suddenly seemed the way to start.

I'm not sure I'm any wiser now than I used to be (maybe more vocal), or any more disciplined—and I don't have toddlers screaming at me! But I have learned that becoming a writer is a life-long task. I've learned there are certain shoulds I've had to unlearn and find other things to put in their place. I've learned to talk back to them the way I talked one night, years ago, to my insomnia, writing a letter to it as though it could listen. "Insomnia," I said, "Why do you plague me?" I let insomnia answer:"Why must you always be in control?" There was some truth in that question. I wrote it down, for my insomnia, went to bed, and went to sleep.

I've learned enough to know my shoulds are not necessarily yours, but they might be. I've learned to listen to what mine are, to talk to them, to let them talk back. What are the shoulds you listen to, Nora? Are there any you can let go? Have you tried talking with them? Inviting them to be on their way? Who knows what they may reply!

THE EAST VILLAGE INKY

AYUN HALLIDAY

I REMEMBER when I couldn't wait to be old. I spent an entire afternoon in the sunless passageway between the neighbor's chainlink fence and our garage, covering every brick I could reach with colored chalk. Squatting to retrieve the yellow stub from the dirt so that all my flowers wouldn't be pink, I had no trouble believing that I was creating an art gallery. Crowds of adult art-lovers would march up our driveway, eager to pay for the privilege of squeezing into that narrow space behind the garage. I would sit by the for-sythia bush, depositing their admission fees in the red plastic cash register I had received for Christmas.

By the time my mother called me for dinner doubt had started to creep in. What would I do in winter, or when it rained? How would people buy the art? I couldn't very well expect my parents to let me disassemble the garage, brick by brick. Even if they were willing, I had no experience with heavy demolition, and the only tools I was permit-ted to use without help were in the sandbox, under a board because the neighborhood cats did bad things in there if we left it uncovered.

My mother called again. I grew up in the kind of neighborhood where women cooked carefully planned meals for their families and children emerged from bushes, holes, and private narrow spaces when summoned, shortly after their fathers' cars turned into the driveways. I had big plans for what would happen to me when I was old. I had a big imagination and no sisters or brothers to tell me that I was a total stupe.

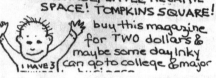

the East Village
INKY no.1

in which the mother of a baby
struggles to reclaim some semblance
of her once creative life by hand-
writing a highly digressive guide
to New York City's East Village
during the baby's naptimes.
FOOD! SHOPPING for SOUVENIERS!
HAIRCUTS! OBSCURE TASTES!
MADDENINGLY LiTTLE NEGATIVE
       SPACE! TOMPKINS SQUARE!
         buy this magazine
         for TWO dollars &
         maybe some day Inky
I HAVE 3 can go to college & major
                           ($2-)

a buck for mommy, a buck for baby. That's enough
for another trip to the photo booth!

Some might say that I held on to my childhood for a good long time. I studied theater and applied my degree to a career in waiting tables. I traveled around Europe, Asia, and Africa with a dirty backpack on my shoulders. The plays in which I performed started at midnight and had no special effect more involved than clicking a flashlight on and off. I got married in a rented loft in New York City wearing striped stockings and a cheap dress, through which, I later learned, my underwear was plainly visible. I wrote poems that I didn't finish, considered plastic milk crates furniture, and had a lot of friends like myself. My first child wasn't born until I turned thirty-two. I'm not an idiot, but I genuinely believed that the baby would spend a lot of time curled at my feet like a kitten. Being pregnant was like decorating my parents' garage in colored chalk, except that now I was the mistress of an East Village apartment only slightly larger and worlds more expensive than their old wood-paneled station wagon. The unsuitability of my situation didn't bother me. I had great plans for the surprise package in my uterus. I took potshots at Barney the purple dinosaur and those ugly toys that play tinny electronic versions of "Twinkle, Twinkle, Little Star." There was no reason why the baby couldn't be my confederate.

Even after she was born, I continued to imagine that I would have no problem partaking of all my established amusements. I would bring her with me! She would learn to turn her nose up at all plastic representations of characters who didn't join Sesame Street until years after I stopped watching. Osmosis would lead her to like what I liked. I like to read books with lots of words and no pictures. That's fun for me. I gravitate to activities that involve holding a pen. I like to sit in auditoriums filled with quiet, respectful people watching other adults on big screens.

Babies don't like these things. You can sneak it past them for three or four months but once they figure out how to crawl, forget it. The older the baby gets, the less willing she is to indulge you. She will use every weapon in her considerable arsenal to prevent your further participation in the very pursuits that once comprised the most meaningful part of your existence. The baby would like to remind you that she is now the primary reason you were put on earth. She will roll over, cry, shit, coo, clap her hands, even grab your pen and jab it into her own eye, if that's what it takes. She does so without guile. As advertised, her gummy smile is irresistible, inspiring fierce pangs in the one who birthed her, but her conversation is far from choice. The little melon farmer will strand you. You have lots of time on your hands but painfully limited options for how to spend it. Your mind gets a bit soft.

I've never been much of a stickler for the housekeeping duties that come with adulthood, but the baby had me in such a chokehold that I felt nostalgic for the days when mopping the floor didn't require hours of strategic preparation. This couldn't be me, absentmindedly swiping puréed yams and cat hair from the floor into my own mouth while waiting for my husband to come home from an exciting day temping at Citibank. I feared that a large and utterly tedious beast would devour me before my first-born child could mount the tenement staircase, pronounce her own name, or eat anything with a texture more robust than wallpaper paste. If it hadn't been for the magazine, I don't know what I would have done. The magazine saved my heinie.

It wasn't one of those glossy mainstream monthlies that publish the same two articles in every issue on disciplining your toddler and decorating the nursery for under two thousand dollars. It wasn't a slick newcomer hyping money management as hip and fun. It sure as bugfuck wasn't Martha Stewart Living. I guess one might call it an anticorporate, consciousness-raising, feminist call to arms, although I feel rather immodest saying so since I write the thing myself. It's not really a magazine but what is known as a zine, a self-published, highly subjective personal periodical with questionable proofreading and a laughably small circulation. But my god, I'm thirty-six years old. Most of my fellow zine publishers are disaffected high schoolers, urgent with the desire to explain why sexism, racism, and the eating of animals are wrong.

I'd always wanted to start a zine. I just couldn't seem to come up with a compelling subject. To put out a zine, you have to find a sustainable passion, something that will drive you to create issue after issue, stapling them together long after everyone else in your house has gone to bed. It wasn't until my daughter Inky turned one that I realized I had something to write about after all. Why, I was no different from Judy Garland in *The Wizard of Oz*! The thing I'd gone looking for was right in my own backyard, except I didn't have a backyard; I had a rusty fire escape that I was afraid to sit on with a baby. I could write about that! Though I sometimes feel like I'm building a sports car out of an empty refrigerator box, making *vroom vroom* noises under my breath as I daydream about driving it down to Mexico by referring to my outpourings as a magazine, not a zine, I can be both self-important and nonchalant. Some people to whom I give complimentary issues aren't sure what to call it, given its humble appearance. They ask if I'm still making my "little newsletter" or "that pamphlet." One woman slightly younger than I am and thrice the adult, always introduces me to her friends with the conversation-stopper, "Ayun makes a zine." The way she says it, it rhymes with "swine." Her friends wrinkle their noses politely, as if they've been told that I play with dolls. She confidently mispronounces my name, too, in the spirit of camaraderie. I'm too sheepish to correct her. I momentarily wish that my name were Barbara and I were redecorating an old farmhouse that my husband and I had just purchased upstate. I don't stay embarrassed long though. That zine keeps my wig on straight when the pedestrian lunacy of raising small children is almost more than I can bear. People who think that it's laughably unsophisticated should see my art gallery.

For my inaugural issue, I took ten sheets of 8 1/2-by-11 paper out of our computer's unreliable printer, checking first that no hastily Xeroxed flyers for our old low budget theatrical endeavors were on the flip side. I scrounged around for a black fine-point marker and found one among the dead soldiers camped in mugs on our desk. I felt as fluttery as a sophomore with a speaking part in *Oklahoma*. The moment I touched the pen to the paper, Inky woke up, so I put her in her little blue backpack and we walked around our neighborhood for hours. The opportunities for rubbernecking in the East Village are endless. I didn't have the money or the disposition to reserve a table at the newly opened restaurant with the heavy buzz, but unlike the other lost souls roaming the sidewalks, I could press my nose to the plate-glass window and gaze until I'd had my fill. The baby gave me carte blanche. Leather-clad couples enjoying seventeen-dollar plates of postcoital polenta impressed each other by cooing at the little face peering in. It sure beat sitting around at home, staring at the congealed blobs of baby food I was too fried to sponge off the walls. We went on safaris in search of intriguing graffiti, outrageous T-shirt slogans, and colorfully costumed madmen. Once we saw a severed chicken foot right in the middle of Avenue A. We saw a pile of what I've come to call "poo-poo" with a spoon sticking out of it. Poor man's pudding.

When the weight on my back began to sag, I raced back to our 340-square-foot apartment, eager to reunite with the paper and marker. I scribbled furiously while she slept, as if the public was starving for want of our published adventures. Just in case multitudes came to the East Village to retrace our steps I supplied addresses. I doodled pictures of the shit with the spoon, homeless punks panhandling in front of the pizza joint, and a squirrel eating a Toblerone bar it pilfered from a stroller in the Tompkins Square playground. I drew myself in my baggy overalls, gasping as I dragged bags of groceries and a megapack of diapers back from the new K-Mart in Astor Place, while Inky clubbed me over the head with the toy we kept tied to her backpack. It took me forever to figure out how to draw that thing, a little geometric structure made of wooden beads and elastic. Every kid in the city seemed to have one.

My printing dwindled to specks of pepper as I tried to squeeze everything I wanted to say into the margins. I was as serious about this as I'd been that day beside the garage, and it was more fun than the time I helped myself to the forbidden hose to make mud pies in February.

When I had covered my ten sheets of paper, I took Inky to a store that sold vintage postcards, Mexican wrestling figurines, and pajamas printed with hula girls and flying toasters. The owner hated children, whose tiny grasping hands posed a constant threat to his merchandise so his unexpected courtesy toward Inky felt like a benediction. "Yours isn't horrible at all," he confided as he broke my ten. He jerked his head toward a customer crabwalking through the narrow aisles after a galloping, squealing toddler. "Those are the ones that give me hives."

I interpreted this to mean, "Yours is wonderful and always will be."

In the safety of his vintage photo booth, I shucked Inky from her backpack and fed three unwrinkled bills into the slot. It was one of the half-dozen occasions since my wedding on which I'd worn lipstick.

In the resulting photo strips, Inky looks gorgeous and plump cheeked, her sparse, slightly ratty hair following the lines of her perfect skull. She is so little, nothing like she is now, an impetuous, lippy four-year-old, dressing herself in a tutu and pink cowboy boots to comb out her pet washcloth with her silver-handled hairbrush, a monogrammed relic of my childhood. Inky's baby brother, Milo, is a dead ringer for the child in those photo booth strips, though his mother is more worn and knowing than that gal in dark lipstick. Four years in the playground with no sunscreen has taken its toll. In those black-and-white mug shots from 1998, I look expectant and, thanks to the lipstick, passably glamorous. A silly striped kerchief that I found in the gutter is perched on top of my head. Not long before, I had cropped my long hair into a pixie cut, the first since fourth grade. I fretted that short hair veered close to matronly on all but the most elfin of bodies, but Inky left me with little choice, yanking my long locks from her backpack perch like she was disciplining an unruly Great Dane. My 'do rag was odd, but it kept the soccer-mom look at bay.

The two best photos became the cover of my magazine, which I called the *East Village Inky* in a fit of inspiration. Because even the most deserving of little magazines are not printed for free, I called my good friend Little MoMo and asked if she could help me print my magazine for free after hours on her corporate employer's deluxe copier. I assured her that I would do all the Xeroxing and collating if she could just entertain the baby. She agreed, and not just because the first issue featured a small sketch of her squatting before a wild-eyed sidewalk vendor on the night she purchased a phone-shaped purse that dials out if plugged in to a wall jack. Little MoMo has been on our side since she attended Inky's unexpectedly arduous birth, when she called another close friend midlabor to announce over my mournful wails, "We're gonna get this little fucker out of there!"

I have a problem with margins, the severity of which was discovered when Little MoMo had to spend several hours trying to align my ten originals face down on the copier's glass so that the copies could be stacked up, chopped in half, collated, and stapled together without the center binding obscuring the last word of every line. My transgressions were far from uniform, and some pages had to be reduced. I had not been able to stop myself from scribbling right up to the edge, even though I knew from experience that I was supposed to leave at least a quarter inch of white space. This shrink-when-necessary technique seemed to work well, until MoMo discovered that it interfered with the chopping. She sliced down the middle of one two-sided copy to create four pages. We flipped the pages over and a center cut made on the front side decapitated the first line of text on the back.

I struggled to amuse Inky, who had decided that this would be the only occasion on which she would snub her beloved MoMo. With the designated child wrangler taking over the controls of the Xerox machine, I was demoted to babysitter. I kept glancing at the wall clock, anxious that MoMo, who already had been here eight hours before we arrived, might throw in the towel. Copying the zine was shaping up to be impossible. I feared that Inky's mirthful shrieks might attract a security guard, who would discover our scam and make MoMo lose her job. Most of all, I worried that I'd have to start over, recreating the *East Village Inky* with rulers and proper margins.

Inky's father, Greg, was called in to help. Little MoMo and Greg have joined forces many times to bail me out. They got me through that bewildering interminable labor. Sometimes I feel like they're my parents, taking charge while I sheepishly make faces for the baby in the corner. After more abortive attempts, Greg came up with the solution of binding the issue with rubber bands: Readers could joggle the pages back and forth to see all the copy. By Greg's rigorous standards this was not much of a solution, but it was literally the only workable option given the raw material. He was hungry, since it was almost 11:00 P.M. After seven years together, he knew I was mostly grasshopper and would settle for something no self-respecting ant would consider. I thought the rubber band solution was great. I insisted on taking Greg, MoMo, and Inky to celebrate at the restaurant of my choice. They were so exhausted they could barely chew, let alone engage in witty adult banter. It was a shame, since Inky had given up the ghost, sprawling beside me on the booth, a napkin spread over her head to protect her from errant forkfuls of rice. I've always been a messy eater. Of course, the bill for dinner far exceed-

17

ed the cost of printing the magazine at a copy shop, though one could hardly expect a Kinko's drone to work so hard figuring out a way to turn ten densely covered originals into a stack of legible copies. They have their own zines to worry about—anarchist screeds, punk rock manifestoes, and semi-arch homages to 1980s sitcoms that budding intellectual snobbery had prevented me from watching.

The next morning I laid out all the stacks of chopped-up, Xeroxed paper on the warped dirty floors of my apartment and assembled them to make a whopping fifty copies of the *East Village Inky*. This felt like a great achievement, given that Inky had a baby's fondness for paper, rumpling great handfuls while sucking a couple of pieces into a repellent, pulpy mass. Several times I untaped her disposable diaper to find a few flecks of homemade confetti planted in the compost.

Rereading my copy, I thought it was pretty good, despite the irritation of having to shift the pages back and forth within the rubber band binding. There were a couple of spelling errors and a poorly drawn hand I'd whited out and never bothered to replace, but I can always turn a blind eye toward my imperfections when fixing them would require much work. Satisfied, I popped Inky into the backpack and struck out for the playground, half a block away.

That was scary. I was about to take the plunge and identify myself as something other than a mother. I'd developed a pretty easy camaraderie with the other parents who used Tompkins Square for their children's recreational needs. Still, maybe our affinity was limited to talking about how much we hated people who could only talk about their children. I had felt a similar flush of friendship for the European tourists Greg and I had

hung out with for a day or two on the beaches of Southeast Asia a few years earlier, and where were they now? Taking a deep breath, I approached Inky's cronies' mothers, carrying some little Xeroxed invitations I'd whipped together the night before. Above a drawing of a baby astride our tumbledown brick building, I printed, "Roof party to celebrate the first issue of the *East Village Inky*." There was barely time to explain before one kid snatched a ball out of another's hands. I was grateful for the distraction. It delayed the embarrassment of outing myself as a thirty-three-year-old who thinks forty small handwritten pages can be rubber-banded together and called a magazine.

People were excited at the prospect of a party. We hadn't yet begun the endless round of toddlers' birthday celebrations where the tofu mommies' best intentions were snuffed out by the weight of chocolate icing. I said that I hoped this would be the opening gambit for us to get to know each other outside of the playground. By the end of the afternoon, I had handed out all my invitations, giving one to anybody whose kid's name I knew. Everybody promised to try to make it, except for one little boy's mother who begged off, saying, "I'm sorry. I can't take him up on a roof. It just freaks me out too bad, what could happen to him on a roof." I knew exactly what she meant, but I could not squeeze more than two or three adults into my apartment. She had a reputation for being a bit overprotective. Her son was a shovel-loving sweetie who had been rerouted at thirteen months from an overseas orphanage. If I had had to work as hard as she did to become a mother, I too might have steered clear of the tops of tall buildings. Instead, I believed in a magical force field that would keep the children from harm, the way I once believed a diaphragm would protect my lady egg from marauding bands of sperm. I told people to bring their strollers so we could restrain the children if necessary. I didn't want anybody to walk or toddle or crawl over the edge in the split second it takes a nursing mother to grab another beer.

The night of the party it drizzled off and on, but that didn't stop them from coming. Huffing and puffing after carrying strollers up six steep flights, they arrived to eat grocery store-brand chips and admire our stellar view of the Empire State Building. I pointed out that if you stood near the stairs and craned your head to the left, you could glimpse the top of the Chrysler Building. Those who braved the edge could observe the final flowering of the lively Saturday night drug trade on East 9th Street. Everyone received complimentary copies of the *East Village Inky* #1.

"What is this?" one mother inquired politely, gesturing to the zine I offered in return for the wrapped gift she had brought assuming that it was Inky's birthday. I was
equally confused. I thought we were all clear on the relative ages of our children. Didn't she remember that her child was exactly seven months younger than Inky, whose first birthday had passed without a party because we were traveling in Scotland at the time?

"Oh, it's just something for you to read on the toilet," I trilled, dancing away to a far corner of the roof. How could I possibly have a child? I was a child, hoping that the grown-ups would make a big fuss over how creative I was.

After a while, enough people were at the party that I could forget why I was throwing it. It was fun to join the adults in making a protective ring around the children. Inky was the only one who was asleep, fastened securely into her backpack. The others sat upright in their cutest outfits, eating Cheerios and quartered grapes from paper napkins. They were the celebrities. Everybody knew them and cooed over what they were wearing. An eight-month-old blonde received a lot of attention over a jeweled bindi dot and braids the size of matchsticks. One little boy was doing laps around the roof, Greg hot on his heels. "Which are his parents?" Greg panted as he passed by. "Can you tell one of his parents to keep an eye on him?"

Actually, I didn't feel I knew the little speed demon's parents well enough to do that. They were probably tired of him. Playground scuttlebutt had it that they were tired of each other, not that we knew either of their last names. On their way out, the father graciously informed me that I had no taste whatsoever for giving Martin Scorsese's latest movie a pan in the zine. Man! At least he was an attentive reader. I hadn't seen a movie in months when my mother flew in from Indiana, offering to baby-sit so that Greg and I could go on a date. Under the circumstances, my pump was primed to like that movie, but that movie, as reported in the *East Village Inky*, was a steaming piece of j.

I talked a lot about movies in that first issue. I included a review of every movie I'd seen since Inky had been born, accompanied by sketches of her nursing in a theater seat and wailing in her car seat as I leapt guiltily from the passenger side of Greg's Dodge Shadow to meet a friend under the marquee of a Cineplex in Chelsea. I also talked about Habib's Place, the three-table falafel joint on our block, where the owner played Billie Holliday and Louis Armstrong and sometimes hired a jazz band to play on the sidewalk. Sitting near Habib's front window on a summer night, I felt as if I were living in a romantic movie about New York instead of in an overpriced hovel the size of a suburban sandbox. I wrote about stores where you could buy green tea ice cream at four A.M., and the dirty Russian Bathhouse on 10th Street. I wrote about how Inky had been pulling my hair so badly I went to cut it all off in one of the three chichi parlors on our street. One stylist had cried when I entered, "Phew! What stinks like Lysol?!" I did. It was me. There was a time when I would have tried to suppress that information, but motherhood had killed off discretion about my body. Before my appointment I had dabbed myself with lemongrass oil, thinking that it would help me resemble somebody used to blowing sixty-five dollars on her hair. Instead, I smelled like the stuff housekeepers more conscientious than I used to disinfect toilets. According to a hip young haircutter in platform shoes, that was worse than smelling like the toilet itself. In the rubber-banded zine, I came clean, announcing that more than once I had mistaken the fancy pomade the stylist sold me for my deodorant stick, ending up with beautifully sculpted armpit hair and a relatively inoffensive head. Hell, nobody wants to read about a perfect mother. I drew a picture of a massive woman I'd seen wheeling a screaming toddler up Second Avenue in a stroller, a cigarette balanced on her combative lower lip. Printed on her T-shirt was the legend Fuck All Y'all! All right! It sure beats World's Greatest Mom.

There was plenty I didn't mention. I never wrote about the isolation and despair that had led to its creation. That first birthday we went to Glasgow for a close friend's wedding and figured that we would have even more fun if we participated in an avant-garde performance workshop the bride's theater ensemble was teaching. We could take the whole trip off our taxes on a Schedule C. We had passed ourselves off as working artists for years, the kind of working artists who buy their own props and costumes, who write plays that make copious use of flashlights because the theater can ill afford lighting equipment. In return for cleaning the theater's restrooms and Xeroxing our own programs, we got a rock-solid identity unsullied by anything so mainstream as a commercial production. I had performed right up to my due date, despite the discomfort of the audience who'd paid twelve dollars to watch me slam my enormous pregnant body into the black walls. That's how committed I was to downtown theater. After Inky was born, I wrote and performed a puppet show about the two weeks we spent in the Neonatal Intensive Care Unit of St Vincent's Hospital. Of course, with a six-month-old baby accompanying me to every rehearsal and work session, I couldn't afford to be caught up to my elbows in wet papier-mâché, so the puppets were played by yams. We were always about making it work. I thought taking Inky to this performance workshop across the pond would more than work, that the presence of an innocent, spontaneous child would inspire my new best-friends-to-be, the international artists who'd signed up to take this playful and utterly inessential month-long workshop.

To my chagrin, everybody thought I was a really good mom. They thought I was a dedicated wife, showing up with Greg's lunch every day, which I started to do when I realized that I couldn't attend the workshop in good faith. Inky's chattering and wriggling disrupted the other participants' process, not to mention my own. I spent hours wandering with my papoose through the iron-colored mist, feeling ostracized, lonely and very very sorry for myself. I believed that nobody knew my name. I pumped Greg for details about the other participants, hungry to be involved, however tangentially, with some kind of adult community. During their lunch break, I held my breath, hoping that Inky would do something cute so that people would be nice to me. When people were nice to

21

at what age does one KNOW IT ALL?

(35?) thought she knew it all when she had one child (as opposed to sr. year of college when, knowing nothing, she operated under the delusion of knowing everything) or when pregnant with her first baby, she held forth as an expert in childrearing — GO TEAM!) Now that she's the mother of two & knows everything again, she fears she's forgetting everything. Like that guy in "Flowers for Algernon" or Irina in "the Three Sisters". She can't remember the function & attachment points of most human muscles or the name of that really cool river town in Thailand or who's running for what political office. She knows how to pick up small pajama bottoms & her husband's discarded socks with her bare feet. She forgets how to write a resume but remembers all the words to the opening theme of "Arthur". (3?) Begins at least

(2? MONTHS) seemed to hold the key to the universe when he was a little butterfly one minute old! Then he moved in with us! Knows how to stare at leaves and lightbulbs for an hour without growing restless. Does not know that a day will dawn when he can no longer go about naked (neither does his sister). Knows which big monkey dispenses the milk. Knows how to smile. Knows only kindness & love. Knows enough to scream in the car seat.

Are you FRUSTRATED?!

2 out of 3 sentences with the phrase "I know that but—". Has apparently learned that monsters are supposed to make you scared. Knows that if mother accuses you of being "jacked up," you can hotly deny it while prancing across the couch cushions, wagging your head back & forth. Knows the alphabet, which subway goes to the East Village, the names of all the minor characters on the Simpsons, how to turn on the cordless phone, the VCR, the computer and every out-of-the-way light switch in the joint, how to simulate a blood pressure reading and how to dress herself. Does not want to know why she can't wear her mittens in August. Knows to shout "Five minutes!" when told she's leaving now.

22

me, I felt pitied and ran away like Cousin Ribby, the most neurotic of my childhood pets, a cat terrified of humans. I picked fights with Greg. I counted the hours until he would come home for the night. I wished Inky would sleep all day. I wished I could sleep all day. I wasn't allowed in the pubs with a baby. I spent many unhappy, boring hours protecting my host's books and CDs from Inky's little paws. I came back to New York in despair that this little daughter whom I loved so dearly was going to cut me out of all the fun stuff I bitched about before she was born, like painting the stage at two in the morning, arguing about aesthetics, and hanging out in unfriendly bars after poorly attended, poorly performed shows. I was an only child from a repressed and fractured home. As an adult, I'd had a taste of belonging, but then I had a baby and got kicked out. The people who kicked me out were nice about it. They smiled and thought I was a really great mother, but they had stage floors to paint.

I had to take the bull by the horns. Instead of shaking a stuffed bumblebee in Inky's face for the tedious hours between her naps, I could take to the streets. I could chronicle the minutiae of our lives. Spotting a pile of shit with a spoon sticking out could be a genuine accomplishment. I would set a roaring example, like Fred Smith, a retired Wisconsin farmer who spent his last years erecting enormous cement sculptures of patriotic tableaux on his land. My family drove by the Wisconsin National Cement Park for many summers, and then a friend and I finally pulled over, looking for some kitschy hipster fun. Fred was long dead and the neighbors who regarded his creation as a folk art treasure had trumped those who thought it was an eyesore. His property had been designated a national landmark and had received a great deal of exposure on Japanese TV. The ranger gave me a pamphlet about Fred's life and his eleventh hour artistic impulses.

Unlike me, Fred was a Midwesterner of few words. Asked what drove him to create hundreds of giant statues on his land, the farmer replied with something on the order of, "People like to look at them and then they like me too." That's valid.

I wonder if dairy farming is so far removed from raising a little child. Both anchor you to a never-ending round of chores that tax your body while doing little to stimulate your mind. You have no choice if you want the living creatures in your care to thrive. They're sweet and without guile, but you begin to crave the company of those capable of speaking in the abstract, people who can understand and maybe even appreciate a book without pictures. You feel like you're alone a lot, although you're hardly ever alone because you're never far from your littlest loved ones and their unrelenting bodily functions. At least the herd doesn't try to follow the farmer into the shower. Still, I can imagine how making Thomas Jefferson, Paul Bunyan, and hundreds of Indian braves out of cement and broken bottles starts to seem like a crucial enterprise. Any attention is just gravy, but you'd be lying if you said you prefer your turkey without gravy.

What rescued me remains as unpolished as one of Fred Smith's pioneer families, eternally traveling in a cement covered wagon. I was thrilled when I discovered that a few hundred people out there were willing to pay two dollars to read about what I depict as a life of tedium and frustration. The best part is hearing from readers, which happens fairly frequently thanks to the miracle of the Internet. Many of the *East Village Inky*'s fans have little kids and as such are attracted to the keyboard as a stalling technique. Every minute hunkered in front of the computer e-mailing a stranger is snatched from motherly chores. It is gratifying to hear from women whose children are as old as I am, especially when they give me the lowdown on what life is like "after the last Mr. Potato Head piece has been vacuumed up," as one writer put it. They say that their kids were and, in some cases, still are every bit as anarchic as Inky is. A teenage single mother told me that she thought of her kid when she saw Inky running around in a crown, Greg's athletic socks, and a pair of black nylon briefs that got mixed up with our clothes at the laundromat. A childless lesbian wrote to tell me that her girlfriend thinks I'm a hottie! Does she realize that sometimes I apply four or five coats of correction fluid to give myself a flattering expression? Oh sure, the zine is handwritten because I didn't want to waste those precious naptime hours figuring out how to use the computer, but I'll spend forty-five minutes on a tiny illustration, striving for that elusive balance between self-mockery and a hairdo that looks far more insouciant on the page than on my head.

Mostly, the text comes easily, since my muse rarely shuts up. She's right there, spoon-feeding me more material, like guns are bad and a crazy man shooted John Lennon with a gun and Oko Nono cried, did you hear about that? Inky says it; I write it down and enjoy doing it. I draw what she's wearing. Sometimes I think I steer her toward some of her wild getups in hopes that someone will e-mail me, laughing that her kid does the exact same thing. It's so heartwarming to know that we're not the only family whose pet has formed a passionate sexual attachment to an inanimate object. Our cat screws a filthy rag doll three times a day. I'm always a bit uptight when Inky has new playmates over to the apartment, afraid their mothers will see the horrid remains of Jambo's doll on the living room floor and assume that it's one of Inky's toys. In the zine, it's played entirely for laughs and Greg is a good sport about the way he's depicted in opaque glasses, seated on the toilet, preoccupied by Stalin and Iron Age weaponry. Once a male reader wrote that he was very pleased to see a picture of Greg wielding an atlatl and he didn't know why the more mainstream press exhibited zero interest in atlatls. I didn't know what an atlatl was until Greg asked me to draw him holding one. I decided that it should look like a boomerang with a spear sticking out of it. I didn't hear from any women about the atlatl. I figured that they had all gone offline to make macaroni and cheese. It's good just to know that they're out there in Bumblefuck, Idaho. We might not see eye to eye on the best place to raise our children, but we are all in the same boat.

I used to think that this expression meant that we all shared one boat, that your paddles are made lighter by the presence of others. That's not what it means. Even on a good day, my paddles feel like they're filled with buckshot. I'm willing to bet that every other mother's do. Shortly after you give birth, most of the activities that defined your identity are suspended to let you mix apple juice, deal with somebody else's snot, and develop a lot of highfalutin ideas about television. You're not being paranoid or melodramatic if you feel like you're the only grown-up in your boat. The kids never leave the boat either, but what help are they with the paddles? Their arms are hardly bigger than celery stalks. Also, as delightfully surreal and repeatable as their beginning syntax might be, their conversation cannot sustain you through the tedious stretches. If it weren't for those little kids waiting for you to harpoon a fish so that they can tell you they don't like fish, you'd go right over the gunwales. You can't leave them to fend for themselves, even though they are the ones who got you into this mess. You're stuck choking down soggy peanut butter and jelly sandwiches in that leaky skiff. The inviting blast of an ocean liner taunts you as it glides by, its portholes twinkling like a string of white Christmas lights. Damn the passenger list of merrymakers in bias-cut gowns and party hats. It's always New Year's Eve nineteen-thirty-something on the ocean liner. Too bad you're missing it. Then, in the middle of some dark night, when you're up, dog tired, struggling to keep your sleeping children out of the bilge water, you notice another crappy little boat a few yards out. And another. And another. The ocean is crawling with boats as crappy and little as yours. Each one holds a mother tethered to a baby, a sleeping toddler or a jacked-up three-year-old still gibbering from an ill-advised late-afternoon sugar fix. We're all in the same boat, all right. It smells like mildewed life preservers. There are millions of these boats in the sea. We shout to each other across the waves. Nobody will get offended if you have to interrupt her mid-sentence to seize your daughter by the ankle before she dives after a birthday party favor she dropped overboard, possibly on purpose.

The *East Village Inky* is up to issue thirteen now. Many things have happened in its pages—pregnancy, meningitis, the birth of my little boy and the collapse of the World Trade Center, but I think the real secret to its success is that not a lot happens. That's why I keep writing it. If my life ever turns into a whirlwind of parties, international travel, and lucrative writing assignments, I'll stop publishing and let *Vanity Fair* take up the slack. Just think, I could sit on the toilet reading all about myself. Now I write about Inky barging in to demand a snow shovel and an Easter bonnet when I'm on the toilet reading about the thinnest, richest murderers in Palm Beach and the Côte d'Azur, none of whose lives resemble my own. I draw Milo crawling hot on Inky's heels, determined to get at least one handful of cat food. The *East Village Inky* comes out in marathon run-on sentences because I can not stop myself from relating an anecdote about my childhood and recommending an out-of-print book mid-description of how we get up and down the subway stairs. The regularity of my quarterly publication schedule is rare in the zine world. Usually as lackadaisical as possible, in this case I find the pledge of punctuality reassuring. Every issue represents another three months in which my family's luck has held. Nobody has had a serious accident or been diagnosed with a terminal disease. Nobody has gotten divorced or needed to summon the fire department. The bad men have kept to the shadows. Somewhere down the line we'll probably see an obituary for Jambo, but bless his black heart, I think he's the only major character the *East Village Inky* can stand to lose and still stay in business. Every non-event that I can squeeze between the margins is proof that life is sweet. Hard, but sweet, like a misshapen butterscotch found under a seat at the movie theater. Hey, if it's still in its wrapper, what the hell? Pop it in your mouth and brag about your good fortune.

THE RUDEST MUSE

LISA PEET

EARLY SPRING, 1999, a Friday evening. My son was going over to his father's house for the night, and I was meeting friends for dinner and a few drinks. I was performing the age-old ritual of removing clothes from my closet, holding them up to the mirror, and replacing them to take out others as he watched, sprawled on my bed. I paired a black silk shirt with a short black skirt, hung the shirt up, pulled out a flashy mother-of-pearl sequined top that I hadn't worn in years.

"You know, mom," said my son with a sigh, "no one wants to look like an old punk."

Here is a fact: No one will ever, in your entire life, tell you the unvarnished truth like a twelve-year-old. These truths are always unbidden and mostly unwanted, but they cut through all layers of crap like a laser. Our children can't really help it. The burden of their embarrassment with us is just too much to bear on a daily basis, and they must regularly lighten their loads. "You shouldn't wear sleeves that show your elbows if you're going to let them go all wrinkly like that," he would tell me. "Our bathroom towels are disgusting. You can see through them." And, probably the worst one ever, one day when he'd met me at my office after school and we were walking to the subway, "A trained monkey could do your job."

Unlike his other pronouncements, which were basically accurate and which I could live with in relative serenity, I was not quite willing to admit how close to the mark he'd hit. "That's not really true," I told him. "You have no idea what I do there."

"You're a secretary," he said.

I corrected him, "I'm the office manager."

"You're a secretary. You used to be an artist and now you're a secretary."

So: Touché, you little shit. Not that I had given up on thinking of myself as an artist, not after a lifetime spent defining myself as one. Yes, I worked in an architectural firm, but whenever someone asked me if I was an architect I always said, No, I'm an artist. That had been my childhood identity, the class artist, when I was growing up. I'd graduated from one of the best art schools on the east coast. And before I had my son, I had actually supported myself as a freelance illustrator for several years. Work trickled in and the rent generally got paid on time. I had been on a ragged sort of forward trajectory, but having a baby stopped me in my tracks.

I was young when I had my son, and was in no way a mature artist. I wasn't a mature anything, actually. At twenty-three, I was enjoying one of those extended American adolescences, working part-time jobs here and there, dragging my portfolio around town, getting stoned every day, and doing little black-and-white spot illustrations for a few hundred bucks a pop. I had cruised through art school, getting good grades but not really working it. Years later, I realized that I was supposed to be making contacts during those years, taking advantage of all the instructors who were giants in their fields, who could help me someday. At the time, it seemed like kissing ass. I was busy running around the East Village with my punk rock friends. This was the early eighties, and for the first time in my entire life I was on the rising curve of something: I was cool, I was popular, I had a circle of hipster friends and we stomped through life in our motorcycle boots and leather jackets, listening to the best music before anyone else did, giving each other weird haircuts in the days when people actually turned around and stared. I guess middle school must have messed with my head more than I imagined.

I got illustration jobs based on my portfolio, and new jobs based on those jobs. In the back of my mind I probably knew I wasn't really going anywhere with my work, but I was having too much fun to care.

Getting pregnant made me grow up in a hurry. I suppose something else might have done it or I would have slowly come into my own as an adult over many years. Or not. Maybe I'd have ended up one of those old punks my son found so deplorable, drawing cute, edgy pictures and trying to pick up twenty-five-year-old art directors. But that didn't happen. Instead, I went through the universal knocked-up-by-mistake cycle: panic, determination, misery, exhaustion, overpowering hot love for the squirmy little creature in my care. Eventually he stopped needing to be held and nursed every second of the day, and I sat down and sharpened my pencils again—and stopped there.

I looked at my work and saw that it was glib. Somehow the universe had shifted under my feet, and what had seemed hip and smart to me at one point now struck me as facile and tight. The Edward Goreyish crosshatching, which had been my specialty, was a byproduct of the focus that comes with smoking too much pot. My lines were hard. My ideas were lacking in a certain subtlety that, on second look, left me vaguely ashamed of everything I'd ever done. I found myself up against a wall that hadn't previously existed.

It wasn't just the time thing, or the exhaustion thing, or even the unsupportive husband thing, because those don't last. Eventually the kid sleeps through the night; eventually he starts school. Unsupportive husbands can become unsupportive ex-husbands. And, after all, motherhood is supposed to put you in touch with your deepest, most sincerely creative impulses, stringing a straight line from your soul to your hand.

Like hearing a recording of your own voice, or seeing a video of yourself oblivious in a crowd, looking at my art through older eyes surprised me and made me uncomfortable. I didn't connect it right away to being a mother. At the time I thought it was because I'd quit smoking cigarettes and had severed some crucial eye-hand-lung source of deep pleasure and creativity. Obviously I wasn't thinking about the matter too hard. I figured it would just come back on its own.

I kept working, but it was like starting to think about where your feet go while you're dancing; you lose all fluidity. I even read Women Who Run With the Wolves, but my deep, matrilineal intuition was not making itself available to me, at least not as far as my artwork was concerned. Maybe I had used it all up on the baby, he was gaining weight and learning to crawl and all that, so at least I'd managed not to screw him up. I just didn't like what I was making on paper. I didn't resent the rechanneling of my energies; I thought maybe this happened to everyone. I didn't know any other artists with babies. I didn't know anyone with babies period. All my friends were artists and they were working, traveling, getting jobs, getting grants. They all still smoked. Me, I was on a different planet, and it was so strange and new that I didn't see much reason why there should be any overlap from my old life whatsoever.

In fact, everything about this new life was weird and different. I just rolled with it. I was a mama now, I did mama things. I pushed a stroller, I showed my boobs in public, I shopped at the farmer's market. In fact, I dug the domestic thing. After years of living on Chinese food, Snickers bars, and beer, I was taking care of someone who, oddly enough, couldn't eat any of those things. So I learned how to cook and discovered that I was into it. I loved planning our meals, I loved shopping and cutting things up, I loved the smell of onions in olive oil. And because I was still, underneath all the good mama trappings, a pleasure hound, I discovered I loved baking, too. Baking was somewhere in between chemistry and carpentry. Every week I took on new projects, starting with my mom's zucchini bread recipe and slowly branching out into cookies, cakes, mousses, candies.

Especially the cookies and cakes, because, I discovered, I could dress them up. I still remember that particular lightning bolt: the cover of a *New York Times Magazine* food issue showing a tray of Babar the Elephant cookies. Babar! With his green suit and yellow crown, neatly outlined in black icing. The photo showed a regiment of Babar cookies, each one like the other and at the same time subtly different, handmade and accessible looking, ready to be eaten. They were sophisticated, but nursery-sweet. I fell in love with the idea of frosting.

I made Tyrannosaurus and helicopter cookies for my son's school bake sales, baby shower cakes depicting free-floating, spiky-haired fetuses. At Christmas, I built a gingerbread tenement and fashioned a marzipan Santa sitting on the stoop in his undershirt, drinking a quart of beer. Frosting wasn't hard to figure out, sort of a cross between watercolor and spackle, and marzipan was a lot like Sculpey, except in my opinion it tasted worse. People were impressed. "Those are incredible!" friends and teachers and fellow parents would say. "You should sell them!" People always think you should make money doing what you're good at, even if the hobby and the reality are miles apart. If you're funny, they say you should do stand-up; if you write limericks on their birthday cards, you should become a copywriter. It's a wonder that satisfied lovers don't suggest you become a hooker. Everybody, *everybody*, told me I should try and market my illustrated cakes and cookies.

So I did, and people paid for them. High-end food stores bought mermaid cookies and marked them up ridiculously, and caterers called to ask if I could make them two hundred doves with olive branches over the weekend. All the parents at my son's snooty kindergarten ordered my birthday cakes.

I wasn't earning a living, really. Between the time it took me to make my sugary creations and the money I spent on butter and eggs, I barely made minimum wage. They were satisfying, though. They made people happy. And better yet, they were completely disposable. As soon as I had created something and gotten paid for it, the piece in question would disappear off the face of the earth, be eaten and shit out and washed away in the sewers of New York, with only fond memories remaining. I had become skittish about having my work stick around to haunt me. When I doodled, I drew on napkins, the backs of envelopes, anything that could be thrown out. I didn't want art that I didn't like dogging my footsteps, making me feel bad. Like Cronos, I had to eat my children.

Eventually, though, the unsupportive husband became a literally unsupportive ex, and I had to get a real job. In my new incarnation as a single mom, I didn't have the emotional stamina to work through whatever artistic block was in my way, and I needed a dependable paycheck. Hence the job that trained monkeys could perform.

I still made cookies and cakes occasionally, and everyone praised them without fail. Therefore, in my mind, they weren't quite art. And yet I refused to stop calling myself an artist. That was the last damned shred of dignity I had left. I continued doodling on envelopes and doing the odd freelance illustration job, if only to convince myself that I wasn't lying.

I kept what I did to myself, though. Or rather, since no one else in my life took the same degree of pleasure from putting me under the microscope, I found myself keeping my freelance work out of my son's orbit. Whereas art directors can come up with any number of ways to tell you that you're not right for their magazine, or that you need to completely revamp a piece, they're not going to ask "Do you have gray hair in the back, or is that a bald spot?" There are lines that most people don't cross. I could handle the everyday brutality of an adolescent's gaze in any other area of my life, but not that one. So I worked at night; I worked in my office. I filed my finished pieces away in envelopes and didn't look at them again.

I've never been good at sneaking around, though. I'm sure he knew that "I'm going to move the car" was shorthand for "I'm going to go out and smoke a cigarette and then buy cough drops at the drugstore." I'm sure he knew that my boyfriend and I actually had sex. And at some point in that year of obnoxiousness, my snide little truth-teller tugged at a manila folder under my arm and said, "Let me see what you're working on." So I showed him.

His eyes widened. "That's really *good*," he breathed. And then narrowed. *Here it comes*, I thought.

"You know," he said, "if you put stripes on that boy's shirt it would kind of stand out more from the guy behind him," and threw me a sideways glance, checking my reaction.

I mentally threw some stripes on the shirt. He was right. "OK," I said, "I think I'll do that."

He studied the drawing again. "And you know what, you could put some ribs on the rubber toe of that kid's sneakers, like I have on mine, and that would look really good." And damned if the kid wasn't right again.

"You know," he said, "I could give you some suggestions for your drawings, if you asked me. I have some pretty good ideas."

At the time, what made me happiest was seeing that he believed in his eye. He'd been artistic and creative when he was little, but it seemed like he had gradually talked himself out of it. I could never tell whether it was because he felt overshadowed by the fact that, when we were down on the floor with markers, I could draw a horse that looked like a horse and he couldn't, or whether I had somehow communicated to him my distrust of my own hand. Because, let's face it, I had gotten him this far with no broken bones, no gaps in his education, no overt signs of malnutrition, but there were actually plenty of ways to screw him up that I'd never dreamed of when I was lying awake, pregnant, panicking. Maybe, I thought, acting as my artistic advisor would be a safe way for him to stay in touch with that side of himself. Then again, maybe he just thought it was a good way to boss me around without getting yelled at.

So I decided to keep him on as my artistic advisor, kind of like having an in-house editor. Most of the people who could be depended on to hire me without much visible effort on my part, worked for agencies that involved children and teenagers, and having a consultant in the right age group was invaluable. "Mom," he'd say patiently, "girls don't wear big t-shirts like that. Guys wear big shirts, girls wear little ones. They like to show their belly buttons."

"Even little girls?" I asked doubtfully.

"Yeah, especially the little ones. Once they get to be my age, their moms start yelling at them about it."

And whereas I thought that the annoying candor would increase exponentially every year until he either left home or I killed him, it started to wane as he got older. Maybe being a teenager made him a little more aware that you don't necessarily want to know every shred of the truth at every moment about how you look, how you act, and the dumb things we are, every one of us, capable of doing.

Last summer, I got laid off. They found an equally well-trained monkey who would work for half my salary, but they were generous with me, and we parted on good terms. I guess I knew it was coming, because I'd been conscientiously working for a while to lower my cost of living. Getting booted from my job made my pride smart for about twenty-four hours, at which point I realized that I'd been given a rare gift: the opportunity to decide what I want to do when I grow up.

Here's a paradox for you: The child gets older, and can do more and more for himself, freeing you for your own ends and at the same time reminding you that you have less and less time to spend with him. At sixteen, my son was fairly self-sufficient. He got up in the morning by himself, traveled around the city by subway, and could be relied on to feed himself fairly well if I wasn't around. My job as prime caregiver was slowly contracting to a few choice phrases: "No TV before your homework's finished," "No Cokes after nine o'clock," and "Did you set your alarm?" Yet the time we spent together was ripening, becoming more precious and interesting every day.

He had so much to say, suddenly, so much information floating around in his brain. He knew world history, he knew about the laws of velocity, he had political opinions that had nothing to do with mine. Our dinner table crackled with energy. He had finally figured out how to express the fact that he knew something I didn't without implying that I was the world's biggest moron, and I think we were all happier for it.

Suddenly I had nothing but time—time to myself while he was at school, time while he was hunched over his computer doing homework. A friend pointed out that unemployment was the poor woman's NEA grant. It was a sabbatical, a reprieve from the constant reshuffling of motherhood, the household, and personal life. Yet I felt even more drawn to be with him when our days did overlap. I finally had a room of my own, a place where I could shut the door and be alone, but the kitchen kept calling. Motherhood wasn't done with me yet.

It occurred to me that I was forcing a bit of a dichotomy on myself. On the one hand, my drawing and painting: Grown-up art, art that required journey and introspection, both of which remained tantalizingly out of reach while I still had a child, no matter how big, under my roof. On the other hand, my illustrated cookies and cakes: Mama art, art that instantly generated approval, warmth, and crumbs. I realized that I was inclined to grant legitimacy to the first because it was that much more out of reach than the second, when, honestly, they are both just points on some crazy eye-hand-heart continuum of mine. I couldn't make food art if I weren't an artist in the first place, and I wouldn't be the artist I am—whatever that is at any given moment—without the part of me that's a mama in her kitchen, good smells wafting from the oven, and my rudest muse hovering at the table waiting for beaters to lick.

Summer, 2003. I cleaned out my desk at work and didn't look back. "So . . . what do you think you're you going to do?" asked my son, cautiously.

"I'm not sure," I said. "I don't know, I thought I might go back to baking and illustration for a bit, see if I can make enough money doing that." Thinking for sure that I'd see it in his eyes: Well, there goes any hope of getting a laptop. There goes our trip to Italy in the spring. And I guess I'm going to have to hit the old man up for my winter coat . . .

Instead, his face lit up and he threw his arms around me in absolute unironic, unteenaged joy.

This was a bit of a shocker. There had been times when I had wondered if he saw me as a decent mother or if he was going to be seeing a therapist for most of his adult life trying to undo the mess I'd made of him. I'd never considered whether he was proud of me or not, whether he had anything invested in my following my dreams.

I never saw his birth as the end of those dreams, and I never, for one second, blamed him for any conflicts I might have with my own creativity. I'm sure he never viewed things that way either. His joy for me, I think, was purely selfish.

Maybe, in some corner of his brain not devoted to physics and debate and teenage girls and Cuban sandwiches, he really did want me to be happy and fulfilled. Then again,

31

MOVIEMANIA MAMA

MARRIT INGMAN

IT'S 10:02 A.M., and I'm waiting. The recorder is wired to the phone, the tape queued. I've readied my questions, e-mailed the publicists, watched the screener, reread my notes, studied the schedule. I have a quarter of a page in a two-page spread. I have two editors waiting. I have nineteen hours until my deadline.

10:03. Will blows his diaper out.

Luck is with me this time. The subject of my interview—the director of a documentary at this year's Austin Gay & Lesbian Film Festival is a father; he has a three-year-old and is charmed by the way my son screams at my aquarium screen saver: *Blub-blub! Blub-blub!* I manage to ALT-TAB over to our Blue's Clues puzzle game and keep talking, though the conversation will be almost impossible to transcribe later. *Bye-bye, Blue!* Will yells.

I can almost hear Glenn Holsten check the clock in his office in Philadelphia. "Blue's over already?" he asks.

My editor cuts that part.

Mother. Film critic. That's me.

The worst part was the pregnancy, when I kept pulling three-hour Iranian film duty. The movies grew longer and more atmospheric as my bladder capacity diminished. The camera would linger in gorgeous wide static shots of the mottled amber landscape; I would twist in my seat and pray for continence. My colleagues chuckled all through the advance screening of *Ali*, for which I required three pissings and one snack (pizza, provided by a theater manager who took pity on me).

I'd arrive swollenly at a preview in my stretch-paneled jeans, and the publicity person would inevitably check and recheck the list. I already stood out like a broken toe amidst the fanboys populating the press corral: the overcoated geeks from *Ain't It Cool News*, the gladhanding hipsters from the cable-access film show, the lanky indie-rock journalism majors from *The Daily Texan*. Even the reviewer from our corporate daily was hunched and male and nerdy and dressed in black. They'd skulk right in, while I ran a gauntlet of questions, addressed to me but directed to my fetus.

"Are you the ad rep?"

"Are you reviewing?"

"Are you *sure*?"

I'm not complaining. I loved it. I'd groan and thrust out my belly and shift my weight as if I were going to drop in the middle of *Not Another Teen Movie*. The weirder the movie, the better the reaction. A studio liaison tried to talk me out of *L.I.E.*, a caustic drama about a teenage boy's relationship with a neighborhood pedophile. I gave it three stars. I also discovered that the studio reps wouldn't try to collar me and squeeze a pithy quote out of me when the film was over. All I had to do was clutch my abdomen and make for the door with a panicked look, and the tight knot of exiting viewers would magically unravel.

Then came the birth, a cesarean that laid me up for a while. My editors sent a gift-wrapped bouncy seat and their best wishes to the house, but I could read between the lines: *Are you available to cover South by Southwest?* It was me or our other freelancer, who was touring with his band. Touring trumps childbirth. I picked up a couple of screeners for the preview issue.

My uterus shrank, but I'd still get the hairy eyeball when I wore Will in a sling to the video store for some cheerful family viewing—*Requiem for a Dream* or *The Sopranos* on DVD. People who were renting Italian cannibal movies and anal porn would look at me as if I were deviant.

I commemorated the release of the dreadful *Jason X* with a *Friday the 13th* retrospective for the paper.

"In this scene Jason puts the mask on for the first time," I'd whispered to the neonatal Will during *Part 3*. I'd put him in the football hold so I could scribble with my free hand, balancing my notebook on the Boppy. "He gets it from that dorky kid who's always crying wolf." Will just nursed.

Once he was consistently alert, I had to relegate movie watching to naps and bedtime. I thought I could get away with watching Vittorio De Sica's *Umberto D.* on video for a column I was writing, since it wasn't violent, profane, or particularly eventful, but Will's infantile dyspepsia interfered. I'd spend day and night shuffling around the living room with a loping, colic-stifling gait. I'd try walking backwards so I could read the subtitles in the back stretch of the room. But he inevitably preferred environments incompatible with the cinema: galloping around the house listening to *Czech Melody Time* or Ministry, driving down the freeway at 70 miles an hour, or angled backward in our recliner with nothing for me to look at but the acoustic popcorn on the ceiling. My column had to wait. My editors exchanged weary glances.

Then two brilliant things happened. One was that Will outgrew his reflux and finally began sleeping horizontally.

The other was the Baby Matinee at our local view-and-brew theater. On Tuesdays at noon you could have your pick of four first-run movies for $5 and a wood-fired pizza for $5 more. The films were multiplex fare—my friend and I saw *Sweet Home Alabama*—but it was a real 35mm print with coming attractions. And Dolby. Will screamed when the lights went dim and the pyrotechnic preview for *The Transporter* unspooled. Then he went limp in my arms and stayed out until Reese Witherspoon's fiancé from Manhattan showed up and the gay best friend tried to pass her off as his cousin. Then Will blew out his diaper.

It was the nudge I needed to get back into action. I wasn't ready for the heavy lifting—an Eric Rohmer series, the twenty-four-hour "Butt-Numb-a-Thon" event—but the fire in my belly was glowing bright.

I returned to the theater as a woman transformed.

The year I spent in the crucible of colic had honed me into a white-hot empathy machine. The faces onscreen sent ripples through the space between us with every movement, every nuance, every beat of a scene. Each scrawl in my notebook was a shout. No, don't kill him! I cried during *The Cuckoo*, a Russian-made war drama set in Lapland. *He's in love! Almost complete silence! Lovely formalist camerawork! The private chained . . . to die!? During The Eye,* a supernatural melodrama from Hong Kong with a *Dr. Orloff*-type premise, I broke the land-speed record for exclamation points. I noted the executive-producer. *(Eric Tsang!)* I noted the plot points. (She's got a brain tumor!) I noted the visual lexicon. *(Double-exposure effects!)* I took down bits of dialogue. *("Maybe I was never meant to see this world!")* Each feeling was twice as intense.

Naturally, I was most unstrung by children and babies in peril. During the zombie thriller *28 Days Later*, my jaded colleagues sat with arms folded while I tried to scramble over the back of my seat. Then the lead actor, Cillian Murphy, stumbled into a farmhouse where a family had died. Their bodies lay on the floor of the kitchen—motionless extras decorated with unremarkable effects makeup—but my gaze lingered on the pallid face of a swaddled baby. *Six months old?* I guessed. *Was she eating from the table? Did she have teeth yet? What was her name?* The sight of a baby conflated my life with theirs, the fictional parents. My milk let down.

After Will's first birthday, I was prepared to reenter the swirling tempest of a film festival. I left Will at home with his father. I put on my laminate and my game face. I fueled up with coffee.

And I walked right into *Girl Wrestler*, a fine documentary about teenager Tara Neal's struggle to stay competitive in freestyle wrestling despite the dearth of female opponents in her weight class, and a statewide rule forbidding intergender matches in high school. Again, my maternal empathy overwhelmed my objectivity. I watched Tara meet her idol, Olympic wrestler Brandon Slay. I watched her face fall when he autographed her T-shirt but said he didn't approve of girls competing against boys. I thrilled when she discovered a practice partner and went to nationals. During each match I sat riveted, my fists clenched with anticipation and my peptic acids churning. I shouted inwardly at the other pushy parents. Lectures spun in my head as I watched contenders of both genders crying, sweating and vomiting to make their weight class. The story transformed me into a frustrated girl, a protective mother, and a furious activist, by turns. Where was the critic?

I despaired of losing my critical acumen. Then I realized that was bullshit. The purpose of film—of any art—is to engage us, to tweak our synapses and set our chemicals in motion: our adrenaline, our sweat. We should not approach it disaffectedly. We should be on the lookout for a miracle, just as we are with our families. Art is an oblique form of communication, like the language of children. We should be attuned to it, and parenthood can teach us how.

I tested this attitude en route to *Pauly Shore Is Dead* (a.k.a. *You'll Never Wiez in This Town Again*), an independent film à clef from the former star of MTV's *Totally Pauly*. My editors had sent me to cover the event, at which Mr. Shore was expected. It was a late-night showing on an otherwise busy Friday; I'd had no reason to expect a crowd of five hundred hipsters too young to recall *Encino Man*, but here they were, jockeying for position in the two hundred-seat theater in hopes of snickering over masturbation jokes and Heidi Fleiss girls. Their laminates outranked mine (journalists are lowly, nonpaying participants). They weren't on deadline and could go skipping out the door at midnight to post-parties and bars while I schlepped home to bang out a four hundred-word cutline and night-nurse my toddler. I was innocent of makeup and bed-headed in a smelly T-shirt and elastic-waisted shorts borrowed from my mom for postpartum wear. I had a cold and a full-sized box of Kleenex. Like my pregnant self, I still felt at odds with my environment. I was not on the lookout for a miracle.

Yet I squeezed in, grabbed a slice of pecan pie and a Schlitz, and listened to Pauly Shore rant a bit about the fickleness of Hollywood before presenting his film—the winner, I feel obliged to report, of a Stony award. It wasn't pleasant to watch, despite the Sean Penn cameo, but I felt at peace after all. I saw that my notes were a balance of motherly superlatives *(Kurt Loder, I love you!)* and healthy skepticism *(Is that really Gerardo?)*. And when it was over, I wandered back to my car in the fresh March air, passing the open doors of nightclubs and bustling restaurants, the bouncers checking IDs. I finally felt liberated from the need to pass as an alternative journalist and let my opinions speak for themselves. I finally trusted myself to be a mother and a writer. I could leak through a zombie movie and not give a shit. I could duck into the Red Fez, order a drink, and enjoy it for the first time, heedless of whether my lipstick was vanishing or whether I was underdressed, whether my congested nose was chapped or my roots showing. Then I could go home to my family, type up my cutline in a silent house, save my work, and snuggle with my son.

It's still a challenge to integrate motherhood and writing. I am still, to my knowledge, the only film journalist in town with a family. I pass up assignments that aren't toddler-friendly (visiting the set of the remake of *The Texas Chainsaw Massacre*, for one) and rarely hand in a feature. Yet, as long as the ideas keep coming, there's hope. I'll find a way. Last week I was grocery shopping when inspiration hit; I grabbed a box of Estee Sugar-Free Rice Crunchy Bars—which I did not purchase—and brainstormed on the back of my grocery list. I've scribbled out thoughts during storytime at the library, using the tiny blunt pencil and scratch paper from the catalog terminal, and stuffed the slips in my stroller basket.

The right people understand. Glenn Holsten concluded our interview by commending me on working creatively alongside a toddler. "It's hard," he acknowledged, "I do it, too." It's hard to keep curious fingers out of the CD-R drive; it's hard to get through a Zhang Yimou epic when naptime is twenty minutes. It will get easier, I know. I can't wait until Will can sit in the chair beside me in the theater. I want to see the images reflected in his eyes. I want to hear him laugh. I want him to experience the reality we share when we gather as strangers in the dark. I want him to suspend himself for two hours. I want us to carry the same sights and sounds in our memories when we walk back out into the light.

TO-DO LIST

FIONA THOMSON

I CAN'T organize this essay; how the hell am I supposed to organize my life?

I could start with all the shit I have to do today:

Wash diapers
Wash yesterday's dishes
Wash myself
Call David back
Call my mom back
Call daycare centers
Process with Anna
Process with my roommate
Work (Somehow two hours of work a day does not add up to twenty hours a week, yet I already can't pay my rent working twenty hours a week.)

But I can't even finish my to-do list. Rudy needs to nurse. Rudy needs to be held. Rudy needs a walk and a diaper change and a new distraction. And so I sit down with her. Or I stand up with her. And I get intoxicated by her smile. Or I get frustrated. Or bored. Or distracted by whatever she's distracted by—green plants, cats, other babies, loud noises.

Then I have to eat breakfast. And lunch. And Anna calls and we giggle, or fight, or talk. Or she stops by to play with Rudy or she stops by to see me and we're happy and relaxed. Or we're not happy or relaxed and Rudy is crying or fussing or sick. Or she doesn't stop by because she is always the one to stop by.

Then I have to do my house chore. This week bathroom, next week kitchen. Then I have to hang the diapers out. Then I have to drop something at work, and get gas, and go to the library. And if I have a babysitter today, and if Rudy takes a long nap, and if I get my four hours in for work, and if I answer all my e-mails and don't get sucked into reading online personal ads or scary international news articles, and if I've already cleaned my room or I've given up on cleaning my room for the week, then maybe I can sit down, take a deep breath, and write.

I don't know if I'm a writer, but I'm trying to write more. I'd like to write. I'd like to spend my time writing. I'd like to be a writer. I am writing right now. Here I am. Writing. Well, typing actually. I am a typer.

A typist I guess. An aspiring typist. One who types. Here I am, a typist, typing and composing the words that I type, so I guess, writing.

And then Rudy wakes up, or the babysitter leaves. How do I pay the babysitter on my part time nonprofit job salary? Very poorly, that's how.

Which is why I ask friends who I can't bear to keep exploiting, or hire teenagers who quit after a week. And I hate the thought of institutionalizing her at such a young age but I think I'm gonna have to put this kid in daycare if I ever want to get any fucking work done, or ever spend time with my girlfriend who is not Rudy's other mommy (nope, this little Heather does NOT have two mommies, she has a mommy, a mommy's girlfriend/secondary caregiver, and a big crew of extended family and friends taking care of her which makes some things harder and some things easier).

Or ever, ever, ever do any kind of creative work like finishing this series of zines on activism and radical history that I started, or this article on fat activism a magazine has actually expressed interest in, or studying filmmaking and making a movie about radical parents featuring interviews with Bernadine Dohrn and Ericka Huggins, or finally getting on This American Life with an inspiring interview with Bernice who should be getting out of rehab soon, or creating a radical puppet show for kids, or learning to throw pottery, or taking a belly dancing class, or learning to weld, or relaunching my aborted porn-writing career that was supposed to be my big money maker and ticket and easy single-mama living. Where was I?

Oh yes, the babysitter is leaving. I didn't get enough hours of work in for the day. I don't have the energy to make dinner. The house is a fucking sty. I have dozens of phone calls to return. I just got a notice that I bounced another check. I think our house has rats again. I can't find my date book so I have no idea if I missed any appointments today. I don't know what I was trying to do today, and I don't know if I did it. I don't know what I'm trying to say in this essay, and I sure don't know if I said it.

So I load Rudy up in the sling or stroller and we go for another walk.

Or we giggle together. Or I tickle her. Or she bites my chin in a happy, contemplative way. Or I hand her blocks and she chews on them. Or I take her outside to touch dirt or

39

TWO WAYS OF SEEING

VICTORIA LAW

a mother-daughter perspective on
photography and documenting history

ON MARCH 15, 2003, I took my two-and-a-half year old daughter Siu Loong to an anti-war march. I brought a three dollar disposable camera, thinking it would be fun to see what she and I chose to document that day. Looking back at those photographs, I see that we not only chose to capture different aspects of the same event, but that we also had a very different way of seeing the world.

EYE-LEVEL

Sometimes I forget that our different ways of seeing extend beyond simple vantage points. From the ground, we focused our respective lenses on what we saw as important and attractive. For me, it was the individuality of each set of protesters. For Siu Loong, it was the overwhelming numbers making up the crowd.

LOOKING UP

Upon hearing the whir of the helicopter overhead, Siu Loong pointed and exclaimed, "Airplane!"

"No, helicopter," I corrected.

She pointed her camera up and snapped. Each time she heard the blades chopping through the air, she looked up and clicked.

Upon first hearing the mechanical whirlybird, I looked up. Had Siu Loong not said anything, I would have paid little attention to it and soon ignored the sound of aerial surveillance altogether.

44

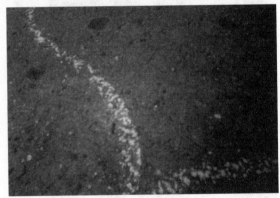

ON THE GROUND

One of the main differences in our ways of looking is how often we look down. Someone less than two feet from the ground notices a lot more than her five foot tall mother does. When I look down, I see small children holding signs, I do not notice the chalk hearts drawn five feet apart along the march's route and the small terrier dog gladly greeting small protesters. The toddler photographer does.

MY ROCK AND ROLL PREGNANCY

LISA MAERAE HINZMAN

IT BEGAN with a simple dream, out of the blue, of two pink stripes on a white, plastic stick. Positive. Pregnancy. My eyes shot open and I stared at the dark ceiling, waiting for my heart to resume beating. Only a dream, only a dream, thank Christ. I slipped back into the comfort of sleep, telling myself that everything was fine, just fine. In the morning the dream hung on me heavily, sending me to the calendar to count days. I should have seen red on Sunday, it was Tuesday morning. No worries, though. God knows I was nothing if not perpetually off-kilter. Nonetheless, I promised myself a chunk of reassurance for breakfast. On my walk to work, I stopped at the Walgreens and purchased a generic pregnancy test, which I took to the bathroom of my day-job immediately upon arrival. I locked the door, tore the kit open, and peed on the business end of a white, plastic stick. As the janitor pounded on the door, my dream came true: two pink stripes, out of the blue. Positive. Pregnancy.

My bandmate and best boy pal, Carl, was within shouting distance, so I shouted. We faked a coffee break and met in the autumnal outdoors, where I dropped my news bomb, burbling tears and disbelief. His immediate response of support, and even happy excitement, saved me for the moment, and I could breathe again. "Now, aren't you glad you quit smoking?" he sassed. Okay, okay, I would be okay. I couldn't imagine going home and spending the day alone in my apartment with this enormity, so I went back to my office to stare at the computer screen and try to sort my head.

How could I, an almost-forty, semi-single rock musician be pregnant? The concept was crazy and the conception was nothing short of a modern miracle. Countless magazine articles had indicated that, at my age, my best eggs were long gone, and I'd probably missed the baby boat. It took months for women who were actually trying to get pregnant to get in a family way, and my little surprise had happened through some half-hearted not trying. So much for my lousy menstrual math. I'd been seeing Matthew for just shy of two months, and had developed a cautious, though very genuine, affection for him, but we were nowhere near even thinking of parenthood. At this point, I couldn't even comfortably refer to him as my partner. And, if all this wasn't enough to send my head spinning right off my shoulders, I'd just spent the past two months booking my band's fall tours. We were to leave for New York in just three days. How the hell could I be pregnant?!

The thing is, I didn't agonize over whether or not I'd have the baby. It seemed all screwed-up, but I'd always wanted to be a mother. And something about it seemed right, so I was going to do it. Later, at home, I found an empty hardcover notebook and started writing to my child: "Hi babe, I just found out about you today . . ."

I wasn't able to see Matthew that night, and couldn't tell him of his impending papa-hood on the phone. That afforded me more thinking time, more time to choose the words, which seemed complicated for such a simple message. I went to rehearsal, and as we played I switched from my beer or three to water, and thought about my tiny one as my bass rested against my belly. Afterward, Carl called a band meeting and I told everyone that we'd gone from a five piece to six. The reaction was amazing. Eena's face shone, unearthly. Steve, blue eyes as big as dinner plates, hollered a happy, "That is intense!" and threw his arms around me. Peter was too shocked to do more than stare, unable to speak, but called the next day to "congratulate the hell out of" me. Within the band there was joy, all told. I knew I was safe with my musical family. It was a good start.

The following evening, finally, after an hour of trepidation and a wanking, improv pedal steel guitar duet, I told Matthew that we were pregnant. The news was delivered awkwardly, fearfully, not as I'd hoped, but Matthew reacted with shock, humor, fear, and strength. "Holy shit, MaeRae," he said, managing a laugh, "that's big news."

Two days later, the band loaded up our white van, Vanna White, our rolling home on the road, and set out for New York via West Virginia. I packed crackers to help keep my stomach on straight, and was granted unlimited dibs on the napping seat in the back.

Our first stop was Cleveland, where we were to spend an evening kicking back with Peter's brother, Jim the Doctor, and Jim's wife, Muffy. The clean house and actual beds were luxe by road standards and we savored the relaxing family time. We gathered in the kitchen for refreshment and chat, and Peter automatically handed me a beer, forgetting for a moment that I'd taken on a passenger. I declined and took the opportunity to say out loud the words, "I'm pregnant" in explanation to Jim and Muffy. I felt like a liar. This was going to take a hell of a lot of getting used to.

The next morning, after muffins and not nearly enough coffee, my four bandmates and I set out, destination West Virginian house party. The hostess was a wild-haired woman with a gleam in her eye and a drink in her hand, beloved and be-sexed by many locals, most of whom would gather that evening at her home to get loud and loaded in celebration of a birthday. This would be my first squeaky-clean gig with child. How very un-tour-like.

The house was a large, rural abode—a wooden palace inhabited and ruled by the artistic sort. There was an apartment on one end of the house, occupied by a young man and woman and their seven-week-old infant. As the couple showed us around their paintings, puppets, and colored glass, I stopped at the cradle to peer at the sleeping baby. He was a tiny perfection, with ears like seashells and a round head, delicate like the egg of an exotic bird. Suddenly, Steve was next to me and put an arm around my shoulder, and we just gazed at the baby, silently thinking the same thing.

Later that evening, I slung on my silver glitter bass and the party began. All around us, the volume went up, and the booze went down as we played. The crowd collectively glowed brighter and danced more wildly with each passing hour, as the air grew blue and aromatic with cigarette smoke and pot stank. Eyes and laughter sparkled, and the loopier and clumsier everyone got, the more separate I felt from the happy chaos. It was odd, but I decided to try to enjoy my outsider's perspective, and imagined how good it would feel to wake up sans headache.

47

The next morning, however, I awoke as hungover as the rest, though my misery wasn't due to whisky and cigarettes, but rather a swirling cocktail of hormones that threatened to rise and go forth should my stomach remain empty. I took to sleeping with crackers and water near my head. T'was a breakfast of champions for the pregnant rock and roller.

On the road again, New York was always a happy smack on the ass for us. Here the gigs were a pleasure, clubs were big-city fun, and we had cool friends in abundance. I made plans to meet my doula friend Jen, along with her mom and her two-year-old daughter, Fern, in Manhattan. A bit faded from the previous night's show, I took the train into the city and met my dear ones at Tompkins Square Park. The playground swarmed with brightly clad children whose hipster, boho parents kept a relaxed eye on them. I shared a park bench with Jen as her mother, known as Granny Annie the Brooklyn Nanny, minded Fern, who had relieved another child of a toy stroller and was pushing it around with authority.

"Jen," I said, "I have to talk to you." She grabbed my arm, looked me in the eye and asked, "Are you pregnant?!" With years of friendship, she could put any psychic to shame and always seemed to know what I wasn't saying. This person at this moment on this tour was a true blessing and a relief, so I spilled words, worries, and joy all over her. She, in her doula expertise, filled me with information and tender thoughts regarding mommyhood, the glow and greenies of pregnancy, and my suddenly very real child. I then learned that she'd had a miscarriage just a week earlier, and I got a new crack in my heart. Still, this was a beautiful autumn day—talking with my Jen of newness and loss, pregnancy and babies. This gush was delicious to me, as I'd been thinking of nothing but my newly occupied uterus and all that meant, and I finally got to roll in this secret part of my life. Too soon the clock pulled me away from Jen and her womenfolk back to the trains, back to another night, another club, another set, another bottle of O'Douls (oh, horrid imposter!), and a new way of carrying myself.

That's pretty much how touring was for me all that fall. My rock and roll self rewritten, going down a familiar old path in new boots that were beautiful but sometimes pinched, finding motherhood between towns and gigs. When a club in Chicago provided us with dinner, Carl made me clean up my rice and beans because, "I don't want you havin' no scrawny baby." In the van, I searched through the weird, prissy, classic, and downright embarrassing contents of my baby name book. Steve asked if he could refer to my fetus as Cletus, until I learned the little dumpling's sex.

In Texas, we stayed with my rock star friend, and I talked babies with him and his pregnant wife. From them I learned valuable, practical bits and pieces, including that the how-to books were worthless and it was perfectly fine to clean the cat box whilst knocked up, all this gleaned from previous experience, thanks to their two-year-old.

I cried the first time we had to pull the van over so I could puke up my Orangina, but I soon became accustomed to wolfing down crackers before going onstage, to prevent turning green. I wrote constantly in my baby notebook, including apologies for road food, "Sorry about that Filet-O-Fish." I was the reluctant partypooper while everyone else took part in the party, but even so, when it was too loud to sleep and there was nowhere to escape to, I still managed to find a partier in a kitchen corner who launched into stories about the birth of his twins, or her fifty-two hour labor. This new dimension of touring had been there the whole time.

Fall touring ended with a grand hometown show celebrating the release of the band's new CD, and, for me, the melding of chick rocker and gonna-be-mommy. I was back home, back to Matthew and my family of friends, about to be back onstage once more for our big show. After soundcheck I saw my friend Delia, a rocker pixie with dyed black hair and a heart too big for her thin body. We collided in a happy-to-see-you embrace and I whispered in her ear, "I'm going to have a baby." She burst into tears and almost dropped her beer bottle, crying for joy. Later, onstage, everything burned more brightly for me as we played new songs to this shiny, hollering crowd. I was learning to play my bass sideways to accommodate my prenatal curvature.

48

THE BLUE PITCHER

PATRICIA KINNEY

THEY ENTER a room like soldiers, marching triumphantly. My blue pitcher, the Austrian pitcher I bought in Germany two decades ago, the one with bubbles in the glass, crashes to the floor. I used to arrange flowers in it—mock orange, rose of sharon, dried hydrangeas. They continue to fight next to the glass from the broken pitcher—another one of my lovely things ruined. Two of them wrestle, scream and say *I hate, I hate,* talk of killing one another as they get closer and closer to the shards, I cry and do not warn them about the glass, wishing they would roll into it, cut themselves, and bleed.

Today I am hand-binding the poetry journal that I edit and publish. Tate, my twenty-two-month-old likes sewing day. He taunts my stacks of journals by rushing toward them on a sudden whim saying, "Wheeee." I try to hold the bulk of a binding session for nap time, but it never seems to work out that way.

I've cut one hundred twenty-five pieces of book binding thread into twenty-inch strips. I've put the pages together in the order that they go. Tate stands across the room.

I am the only woman I know with six sons. Actually, I am the only woman I know with six children. It was normal when I was growing up for families to have this many kids, especially since I grew up Catholic. These days, people stop and stare. They ask me if I know what causes pregnancy. I wait for them to ask if I am Catholic or Mormon. I answer "no" to both questions. When I feel I am at the point where I can make them feel the most uncomfortable, I simply offer that I really like sex. They laugh, nervously.

My oldest son is a senior in college. He will graduate from the University of Washington in less than two weeks. He called home this morning to ask if people send out announcements when they graduate from college. I told him I thought they did, and that he should have ordered some several months ago. He asks if I can just make some on the computer. I say sure.

I have to wash the baseball uniforms for my ten- and twelve-year-olds because they both have games this evening. I have never heard of the fields they are scheduled to play on. Some parents know the names of all the fields; I don't even know the name of the teams. I go to every game I can. With two of them playing on the same nights, I have to alternate my time in the stands. My seventeen-year-old is going to mow the lawn after school, but, before he can, I must fix the cable on the lawnmower. I pay him twenty dollars. I have a mowed lawn and he has gas money for the week. My nineteen-year-old son is six hours away at college. I don't hear from him much. I have not sent him one card this year. I didn't send him a Halloween treat or anything for Easter. I almost cry when I think about him being so far away from home, and how I don't go out and shop for little things to send him. How he never gets a package from home when he goes to check his mail in the dorm.

Earlier, I had all the pages of the journal laid out on my coffee table and one wooden chair. It's an assembly line. Find the cover, find the blank page that gets inserted next, then the information page with the publishing facts and address for submissions, and next comes the table of contents. I sit on the couch and start at one end of the line, making sure that each folded paper envelopes the one before. Tate stands across the room with a sandwich bag full of Lucky Charms. He picks out the marshmallow treats and drops the cardboard-like kernels of plain cereal on the floor. Sesame Street is on television but he is more interested in watching me. I am his entertainment. He comes closer to the coffee table and says, "No, No," echoing what he hears from me nonstop, 24/7.

Now it is time to actually sew the journal. Again, Tate stands closer than I'd like him to. I notice that his golden-blond hair would better be described as dishwater or dirty-blond. When did that happen? He is wearing a red and white Hawaiian shirt and Levis. The bottom cuffs of his pants hide his feet. It looks like he is hovering in the air on hidden stilts. I put my silver thimble from my mother on my right index finger. Tate sticks his fingers out to be crowned with thimbles. He probably would like a silver thimble on each digit, but I only have one extra that I went out and bought yesterday, knowing that he would want his own silver thimble attached to his little finger.

I take a piece of thread and run it across a piece of bee's wax. The wax coating makes the thread more manageable. Tate wants a piece of thread. I give him one. He's says, "Ohhhh, mine." I thread the needle. He must know that he can't have a needle, because he ignores this step. He is watching Elmo over his shoulder. Watching Elmo talk to Dorothy the Fish.

I splay the journal on my lap, face down, and poke the sharp end of the needle through the portion of the book that folds. I pull the needle through, leaving a little over an inch of thread on the inside. I come down through the outside of the back of the journal, poking the needle through to the inside. Tate is watching me again while he takes his string and plays with it in his hair. After I bind a dozen books, Tate comes over and takes my hand. He does this when he wants something from the kitchen. He makes an urgent "uh, uh, uh" sound. I set aside the journal I am sewing and follow him to the kitchen. He points at the cupboard and I pick out the box of raisins. He wants raisins in a Dixie cup. Easy enough.

I walk back into the living room and Tate follows me. Now he wants to sit next to me on the couch while I sew. He wants to touch the journals I have already bound. I tell him he can't touch them because he has raisins on his hands. He dumps the raisins on the floor between the couch and the coffee table. I leave the raisins and shuffle my feet a few inches to the left of them. I'll pick them up later, or one of the older boys will. I don't want to stop the momentum I have going with the binding.

Now Tate finds a bag of chips his brothers left on the living room floor the night before. He holds the bag high and pours the chips into his mouth. Most of them land on the floor.

At one point, I wonder how many journals I've bound and with him we count them one by one. We've sewn thirty-five in two hours. Time for Tate's nap.

While he is asleep, I sew for two-and-a-half hours, uninterrupted. I finish the stack of journals and begin to address envelopes for my subscribers. I also send out the contributors' copies and bundle the stacks that go out to bookstores. It's 2:00 P.M. All I've had all day is a double latte. I pick up some of the raisins off the floor and eat them.

I want Tate to be a part of this thing I do. I think I missed the mark with the rest of my kids, always too busy to stop and let them participate. I kept them busy with their own activities and didn't invite them to be a part of any of mine. My back aches from bending slightly while binding the journals. When Tate wakes up, I will get him out of his crib. He'll be smiling and his hair will stand on end. We'll stop in the kitchen and I'll grab a slice of American cheese from the fridge. I'll fold it in half, then in half again, giving him a square of cheese to eat.

I hear Kellan's bus stop at the end of the street. Tate hears it, too, because he rushes to the window in the front room and bops up and down, excited to see his brother. When Kellan comes through the door, I get after him for wearing his dirtiest tennis shoes to school—the ones even dirtier than his dirty ones. Kellan says he is hungry and gives Tate a hug. I tell Kellan that when Tanner gets home we have to go sell the journal to the bookstores downtown. Five copies to Orca Books. Three copies to Last Word Books. Four Copies to Traditions. Three copies to the retro thrift store, Dumpster Values. The kids think it is fun when people buy the journal. They like to hold the cash or checks we collect. They are amazed that people pay for something we have put together with our own hands. The little bit I make off the journal is pretty much eaten up by postage fees and other publishing whatnots. But, I will make enough extra on this day to pay for Tanner's baseball trophy—ten dollars, due after tonight's game.

Tanner bops in from school thirty minutes after his brother's arrival and airmails a kiss to my cheek. He throws his backpack on a stack of bound journals and says "oops" when he realizes his mistake. The covers of three books end up bent. I pull them from the stack and stick them in the box holding Tate's books, paper, and crayons. He will enjoy drawing on these reject issues. Tanner brings a too-full glass of milk into the living room. A splash of white hits the coffee table. He repeats his earlier "oops," and grins.

I feel the day riding on my shoulders, hanging onto my back. I realize I haven't even taken a shower yet, or brushed my teeth. Kellan remembers he has forgotten to stay after school for a tutoring session he signed up for. I remember writing deadlines which hang over my head like clotheslines full of wet, dripping towels.

*　*　*

My mom was there every day when I came home from school. There was always a snack to eat and someone to tell how my day went. She didn't incorporate my brother and me into her work or projects. She put away her paperwork or sewing, lay down magazines she was reading, pretended like the television was just on for background noise. When we got home from school, it was mom's cue to get dinner ready so that it would be served the exact time my dad walked in the door. He'd only have time to wash his hands before she'd yell, "Pete, come and eat." Mom had odd jobs that she tended to. She was the book-keeper for the local fire department. She was the secretary for our small water district. Jobs she could fold up and put away when the kids got home from school.

*　*　*

It is the bottom of the sixth inning, and there are two outs. Tanner is up to bat. I've taken Tate over to the playground adjacent to the ballpark because he is fussy and would not sit still. I've missed the two innings that Tanner pitched.

I climb up and stand on the top of the big toy, holding Tate in my arms, hoping to see what Tanner does. On the fifth pitch, he strikes out and the game is over. I see everything, and I also notice Tanner scanning the spot in the bleachers where I'd been sitting.

"I'm glad you didn't see me, Mom," he says. "I struck out." On the way home, we stop at the grocery store. The boys try to decide between frozen pizza and frozen waffles for dinner. I see a bouquet of sunflowers protruding from a black plastic bucket near the check stand, pull them from the water, and place them next to our purchases.

After coming in the door, Tate drops down on his belly and eats the cereal off the unvacuumed carpet. Sunflowers in hand, I recalled my broken blue pitcher.

MADRE DE BAILE

KRISTINA JORDAN COBARRUBIA

IN FLAMENCO, the Spanish gypsy art of music, dance, and song, there is something called duende (do-en-dayh). It's a magical, elusive moment, when everything, the dancer, the guitarist, and the singer are all moved by each other and moving as one. It's fleeting, but when it happens, everyone can feel it, including the audience.

However, even though I'd studied flamenco for ten years, duende eluded me. I was good at dancing flamenco, I'd learned the techniques well, but that special, magical feeling was something I'd only observed in other dancers. Just for a brief moment here or there in major concerts I'd see, a performance would suddenly crystallize, bringing the audience spontaneously to respond "Ole!" I would watch in appreciative wonder as the dancers became one with the guitarist and singer, and me in the audience too, swept along in their creative fire.

But I, myself, was just going through the motions. In classes, the teachers would yell at us students to give them more—more energy, more feeling! So we'd pound our feet harder into the floor, but really, what did they want? It's like your first orgasm. Until you've had it, nobody can really explain what it is. So I was following the steps, trying to improvise when the music or singing didn't go where I expected. Like jazz, flamenco is highly improvisational, with a clearly defined structure that can nevertheless end up in any number of different combinations. For a non-gypsy beginner, this can feel out of control and terribly frustrating. For a type-A personality like myself, it's almost a death warrant.

But, eventually, a few years later, something began to click. I'd finally had enough training that the trips and turns of the music didn't throw me. I knew a lot of options in case the singing stopped here, or continued on to there. I'd been to a couple workshops where teachers noticed that I had something coming out from inside, and I felt it, too. Something was there, underneath the surface, thrumming in my heart. It was inspired by the music, mainly the plaintive lament of the singing. Finally, I knew these songs. Not the meaning of the words, my Spanish is still regrettably minimal, but the meaning of the music. It was there beneath my skin.

Then I had my first child. A little girl, the only girl grandchild in the family. At first, it felt like my pregnancy would be a career-killer. All my form and technique blasted by morning sickness and a humongous belly! Would I ever regain my shape and skill? But after my daughter was born, I slowly picked up the pieces of my dancing, recreating my solos from videotapes, and discovering the benefits of weight training. Before long, a new teacher came into town. He'd visited once before, and had liked my style. Now, he was back to do a series of shows and wanted me to be a part of them, including a matinee especially for children. I was thrilled. I'd be dancing a duet with another young woman to siguiriyas (sih-gear-ree-ahs), one of the deepest and most serious songs in flamenco.

Siguiriyas is about loss, loneliness, and sorrow. It has a strong, compelling beat, especially when driven by a hammer on an anvil, as the gypsies used to mark it when they worked in the mines. I prepared backstage as usual for the matinee. My husband would be bringing my two-year-old daughter to the performance for the first time.

I made my entrance from stage right. I crept from the wings, dressed all in black with a poison-green shawl, in sync with my partner entering from the left. The beat was slow and heavy, and I filled my body with tension. This was not a dirge, but a dam, ready to break. We did the first call (a sharp footwork break in the rhythm), stopped, and then the singing began. I moved with the song and saw my little daughter, just the outline of her, dimly lit from the stage lights, her little body standing in the aisle to watch her mommy perform for the very first time.

And suddenly it flooded me. My love for her overwhelmed everything else. In that moment I was not worried about the steps, or my form, or the show. My arms took on new life, new force. Though dancing slowly, each fiber of my being was awake with energy, and passion filled my heart. I heard cries of "Ole!" from the other artists and I realized, this was it! This was duende! The catapult of feeling that projects you solely into the now, the very moment, all your concentration changing into the essence of pure presence. The song filled my body with a fire of spirit, and I felt so intensely I thought my heart might burst. This is what they'd all been talking about, and it had happened to me, because of her, because of my tiny daughter, watching her mommy dance for the very first time.

Of course, nobody mentioned this to me before, but afterwards I heard that a flamenco dancer's performance often deepens after they have a child. Somehow, motherhood grounds you, brings you closer to the earth, closer to blood and pain and emotional truth. Flamenco is a deep and earthy art form, connecting you to the stage or the dirt beneath your feet. And at the same time, parenthood brings your feelings close to the surface—the constant joy of your child's existence, the constant fear for their well-being.

Motherhood does this to you. It brings your emotions from deep beneath your skin, and you end up wearing them on your sleeve. Sometimes, this can be embarrassing, like when you cry during a Hallmark commercial. But in flamenco, it's freeing.

Motherhood opened the door of my heart. My artistic expression has soared. Duende is now a part of me, waiting inside the lilting twists of the singer's melody. My ability to feel and to express those feelings is a current running in my veins. I have only to think of my daughter to tap into it and be swept up in the river of feeling, of life, of joy and of pain so intricately mixed as to be almost inseparable from each other.

ITALIAN SUITE

ROSE ADAMS

BLACKBIRD

Blackbird singing in the dead of night,
Take these broken wings and learn to fly
all your life

On the way to the airport
I sing this for you, my son,
who calls it the crow song,
while we pass wingspreads
that sweep the air
and shadow the land
unlike the dead crow
stuck on the combine painting,
Rauschenberg playing with crow and sky.
It's my song for this trip as we cross land and ocean
to a place you have learned to say
with utmost clarity—It-a-ly.

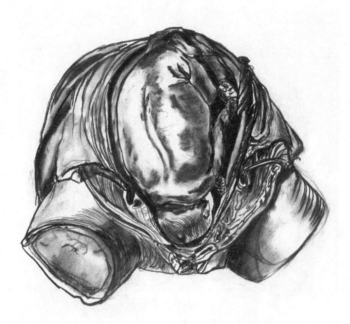

Enroute the monkey puppet pops up
over plane chair backs
playing monkey see, monkey do.
In the Gatwick airport,
the black and white pint-sized soccer ball passes
under tables of lattes and black briefcases
of those who travel without children.

Finally, in Florence
instead of paintings, chapels and tombs,
we search out and pat horses with feed bags
over their noses
in the Duomo Square.

At one of the three Florentine
old family restaurants
you eat your favorite Italian cuisine,
pasta with cheese only, please,
and orange juice in big beer jars.
Guido, the owner, gives you the restaurant's card,

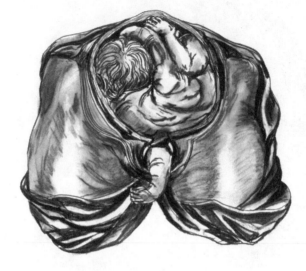

which you turn around and around and then you say it says,
"Play soccer until it stops raining."For hours we play I spy with my little eye
and you ask, "Mummy, why are there so many boy
angels in Florence?" as Raphael's cherubs stare
out from every postcard kiosk.
While I gasp at Gentileschi's *Judith and the Head of Holofernes*
you sleep in a stroller through the Uffizi.

When you dropped one of your two dinky cars
into the road and it spun and wheeled
down the slop through the grate
into the sewers of Florence
daddy lifted the sewer
and put his arm in up to his shoulder
in sludge and putrid feces
then we washed and washed the car
and used enough baby wipes on daddy's
arm to make flags to line a street
for all of Florence to hear
our cheers of victory hoorays.

You say you want to go to a toy store
and we search and search and when we find one
you walk in, turn around, not looking at the toys,
and say, "But where are the children?"

The search for a playground full of children
takes over your agenda
and finally, a half an hour in the large swimming pool
in the centre of Florence makes your skin shine
and you are so happy in the ice cream shop
with flavors you've never known before
and you call any ice cream with more than one color
birthday ice cream because I had bought
three coloured neapolitan
for your four-year-old party.

The best part of Venice
was riding on the Eurostar
then daddy watched you tumble
for hours in the playground on the site
of the Venice Biennale while I tried
to find pleasure in high-tech art,
and for a Euro in San Marco Square
instead of the fifteen Euros a beer would
cost I watched you
re-teaching me ways to play
other than with paint and words,
while you stood feeding the pigeons
flying over, around, roosting on your arm,
seeing you surrounded by hundreds of flapping birds,
the pleasure of a little boy
handing out grain for each one.

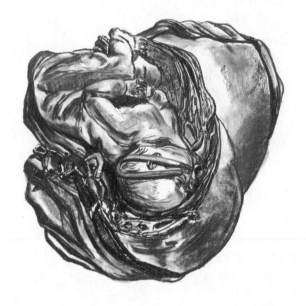

TRANSITIONS

Alarm rings at five, flight at seven.
The morning my husband and son leave me
so that I may move
into my artist identity
I'm stranded.
As we leave, we can't find the key,
unpacking bags, clothes swirl,
trying to put them back they're larger,
my stomach spins,
in t-shirt and panties
I lift my sleeping son,
a shape of a skeleton key branded
deep red into his skin.

Waiting for the taxi in the tall
doorway on the narrow cobblestone
street at 5:30, 5:45 and 6:00,
the large black knapsack

too large for me to lift
slung on your back
as if you're lugging a bag of avocados
up the hill from the farm.
You push our son in the stroller,
I carry the hand luggage,
and we run, my loose breasts flapping,
racing to call a taxi at the fancy hotel.

Too fast for tears you're gone,
I return to my room empty
to slide into sleep for one hour
changing clothes, room, and role.
Fading into a white sheet chrysalis
the locked phone outside my room is ringing
and ringing and I think, "What idiot is calling from what time zone?"

At 7:00 A.M., a pounding on my door
my husband speeds into the room,
"I have your passport, not mine,"
my son in his arms, face glowing
because the taxi is a racing car driving to
and from and now to the airport
and we switch in less than thirty seconds
and my son waves "Bye Mummy," his figure
already receding, two trains passing,
switching lines.

At the museum, I gather my easel,
portfolio of paper, drawing supplies
followed by five museum staff.
An office chair appears on which to sit,
another for supplies. I feel them watching my back
as I set up the Italian travel easel
I bought in Canada
and brought to Italy.
Not used to its bolts and latches
I set it up as evenly as possible,
when I turn to say thank you hoping they will leave,
it crashes,
the bolt on the back not quite
tight enough
just missing the precious
terracottas that I am here to draw.

My lines that day shy,
my stomach and hand still moving in circles.
Later, alone, taking a cab north,
I discover the large playground
with a carousel spinning around
and around that my son searched for the whole week
when he was here.

DAY TWO: DRAWING

Which line do I draw?
The solid wall ceramics and waxes
need to become lines as fluid
as fountain water on my page.

Checking the machine for humidity,
the temperature melting hot
in this room of waxes.
I remember the wax of my childhood,
Blanche dipping rheumatoid arthritis hands
twice a day with hopes for healing,
making perfect replicas of every joint.

The first bulging pelvis I draw
fine lines of uncertainty and the patience of birth
not sure how to ground
the image on paper.

When I draw a small baby's head
protruding from the body
and I sweat like giving birth
in this forty-degree heat,
I think of you, my son
emerging blue from my body.
There are nearly tears as I draw the baby's head,
I thought I was never good at faces
but this one I know.

Later, walking to the station,
what moves me most is a toy store,
the window full of metal trains,
no plastic, only exact replicas of those you love.

ON DRAWING

Working in a room with no windows open
a shade screens the light
to protect the waxes as I draw.

Waxes made for instruction
an unchartered area
when no corpses of pregnant women
could be found.

"Let's get out of this horrible room."

In a glass case beside me
a leather suitcase of early surgery equipment,
a speculum large enough to open a child
to a whole world.

"This is for your mum. This is her
department."
"Kids, walk right through this room
without looking."

After several days of really looking
at these little faces pushing out of wombs
I want the viewers to love them
and I begin to protect them
like my own child
on a playground.

"A Breech is anything, butt or feet
coming first."

Drawing a child projecting
from the uterus backwards
head on straight
listening to Jane Sibery's lullabies,
can't get the leg in the right place
placenta as pillow and wall.

Another line,
another baby born
wrenched onto the earth
with charcoal forceps,
the fine black charcoal powder
falling in a heap around my feet

"This is how you were born, with
forceps."
"No we don't use forceps anymore."

The worst are the ones who whisper.
Don't they think their whispers disturb
or is it that birth for them is as private
as discovery?

"I don't know how gynecologists
can have any sexual appetite
after working at that all day."

With each cast of a child I draw
I feel the intimacy of really knowing
in the way one knows ones own child.

64

SPACED OUT

DEWI FAULKNER

THERE'S NO place for me to write.

I understood and accepted this when we lived in our miniscule apartment in Woodland Hills, the one that had a jail cell amount of natural light, the one that was all hallway. I couldn't carve out a place for myself there, none of us could. My husband, son, baby daughter, and I just floated along in the stew of tables, chairs, desks, beds, cribs, books, bookshelves, videos, video games, toys, toy boxes, toy bags, bath toys, blankets, binkys, diapers, wipes, crayons, pens, papers, files, bills, clothes, dirty clothes, and Cheerios. A lot of Cheerios. At that apartment, it made sense that I had to use the space under my desk if I needed to get in a little writing time. That I had to spread out a blanket on the floor, hang another one over the desk, and use the inside "walls" of the desk as a bulletin board.

As home offices go, it wasn't very comfortable, or sturdy. Within no time, the kids learned that they could bash down the front blanket, stomp in, and wad, shred, and chew through several weeks' worth of work. Little toddler tyrant tornadoes whirling a path of devastation and sopping-wet essays. Much of the time I didn't mind. Much of the time I felt the writing deserved to be ripped up and spat upon. Sometimes, when the kids didn't get around to it, I would do the job for them.

But that was then and this is a three-bedroom house in Van Nuys.

A three-bedroom house that is all windows and open space. A three-bedroom house that my husband and I fell in love with the moment we first set eyes on it. A three-bedroom house that has a miraculously affordable rent. There's a room for toys and books, a room for the kids, and a room for us. There's a back and front yard, a detached garage, and a long driveway, roomy enough for bicycles, tricycles, and skateboards. There is even, I kid you not, a white picket fence.

This house has plenty of space for me to work. So why can't I find it?

My writing habits haven't changed a lick since we moved, except for the fact that the desk I used to hide under broke. So I've been staking out various nooks and crannies, commando-style, tearing down and setting up new posts each time my kids discover where they can find me, should they need a juice box.

It's Saturday, around noon, and I'm sitting at our new dining room table—a risky move, because I'm out in the open, an easy target. I'm trying out this maneuver against my better instincts. My husband tells me I'm silly to scrounge all over the place looking for hideouts, so here I am. He insists he is perfectly capable of keeping the kids occupied and quiet in another room while I write. We'll see how it goes.

I spend the first three minutes trying to make a coherent sentence out of the mish-mash of notes I jotted down earlier this morning while making the kids toast. I spend another three minutes angrily scratching out both the botched sentence fragments and the notes themselves. I write a few swear words in bold, capital letters, even though "SHIT" and "FUCK THIS BS" don't really match the tone of the essay. Seven minutes in and I'm looking for some distraction.

My husband pauses from picking up the Legos in the hallway to watch me grimace into space. He goes into the kitchen and returns with a glass of water and the medication I was supposed to take three hours ago. I hate those stupid pills, and I tell him so. I tell him they're making everything worse, and that if he really loved me he would let me be who I am and not try to mangle my personality with evil poisons concocted within the bowels of Western medicine. I'm trying to pick the scab off of an almost-healed argument. I'm not really mad, I'm just looking for a good excuse to throw in the towel on my essay—it's for shit anyway. I'm an awful writer, a terrible writer; I'm not even fit to hold a crayon.

Seeing that I am trying to climb out of the foxhole and flee the laptop, my husband puts his hands on my shoulders, kisses the top of my head, and says, "I know honey, we'll talk about it later, you get your work done while you have a chance." Stupid loyal, supportive husband.

Despite the valiant effort, my husband's brief foray into the kitchen left the playroom unguarded, and our little prisoners are already on the lam.

The kids, jumping and bopping around my chair, snap me back into reality. The clock is ticking. Fifteen minutes down, and besides a chunk of some pretty foul language, I got nothing. I try to decipher a couple of the crossed-out sentences to see if they are salvageable. It's a lost cause; I don't even remember what my train of thought was. The kids beg for a banana in perfect unison. It's a little creepy. My husband laughs and heads back to the kitchen, "That's something," he says over his shoulder, "whining in surround sound, we should call Dolby."

In the interest of time, I ignore this so-so joke and try to step up what was supposed to be the original plan. "Hey Jon, aren't you going to take them to the park?"

"They don't want to go," he says, returning to the Legos.

"What do you mean they don't want to go?" I say, pushing the notebook aside. "Of course they want to go. Brooks just told me he wants to go."

I call our son over. "Brooks, do you want to go to the park?"

"Yeah!" He always wants to go to the park. He's five. If he had his way, he would live at the park. He also wouldn't wear clothes.

I give Jon a "See?" look. He holds up a finger to indicate that I should watch what is about to happen, like he is a magician preparing to perform an especially impressive parlor trick.

"Gabie," he says to our two-yea- old girl, "do you want to go to the slide?"

"NOOOOOOO!" she shouts back at him, tugging the sides of her hair, as is the cus- tom when somebody pisses her off.

"Come on Gabie," I say, using my best good-mommy-lullaby voice. "You don't want to go to slide, and play and go in the big circle?"

Again with the hair-tugging and, "NOOOOOOO!" And then she elaborates, "No slide! You are so naughty Mommy!" Then she wags her finger at me and bursts into tears. Yesterday, we received this exact same speech because we couldn't take her to the park.

I stare at her, crumpled in a heap on top of the Legos that I could swear Jon just picked up. Now it's my turn to be on the receiving end of the "See?" look.

"Well, you can't go by her," I try, "Gabie's crazy. You know the beast, she never makes any sense." Due to both her independent nature and impressive ability to form complete sentences, I occasionally forget Gabrielle just turned two.

"Okay. We'll try," Jon shrugs. "Come on guys, into the bedroom." The three of them tromp down the hall. I feel like planting a flag into the middle of the dining room table. That's one small step for Mommy.

Thirty-five minutes. I'm golden. I pull my notebook back in front of me and try to decipher my original notes under the scratches. I can't make out anything, so I close my eyes and try to remember what it was I was thinking about while I made breakfast. I open my eyes and stare at the blank laptop screen. I think of what a cliché I am for being a writer staring at a blank computer screen. Jon and the kids pass by on their way out, and I give assembly line kisses to all three, except Gabrielle. Displeased with my quick kiss on the top of her head, she sticks out her face, turns up her little nose, and waits for me to kiss the space between her nose and her upper lip. By the time she has decided she has received a sufficient number of smooches, Brooks and Jon are already outside. "Wait for MEEEEEEEEE!" Gabrielle shouts, running into the kitchen and pushing her way through the half-closed back door.

I hear my family's shouts and laughter get quieter and quieter. I decide to plunge in, sans notes, and remember as I go along. I try a little free writing. Two sentences into my consciousness' stream and I'm already going back and editing what I have written. I take off my watch and set it down on the table. I rub my arm. I stare at the veins on the under side of my wrist. Ugh. I hate veins. I'm down seven minutes.

*　　*　　*

Sometimes life happens even in the middle of an essay.

I have just returned home from UCLA hospital's acute psychiatric ward. I have bipolar disorder, and about a month ago had a nasty reaction to a medication my psychiatrist prescribed to curb a severe depressive episode. During the two weeks I was supposed to give the medicine a chance to "kick in," my symptoms worsened significantly. Not only that, this medication that was prescribed to stabilize my mood actually added to the bouts of mania that had me chopping off my hair, accusing Jon of trying to steal our children, and clawing up the dirt in the backyard. After one of these fits, I would I walk into the bedroom and promptly fall asleep. I know these things only from what Jon has told me; I don't remember a thing. He also told me he managed to keep the kids away, that they didn't see anything. Although, they probably heard some yelling. I remember having some awareness of not wanting to scare the kids, and I have faint memories of them coming into the room while I was crying or sleeping. I remember that I would wipe my eyes and play with them for a bit. I remember telling Jon this was proof I wasn't that bad off, that I still knew how to act in front of the kids. The only reason I agreed to let him take me to the hospital was his threat that if I didn't go willingly he would call an ambulance.

"You would do that to our kids! You would let them see their mother taken away in a scary truck with sirens!" I shouted.

"Absolutely. In a minute."

Thank God for that threat.

I spent a week in the hospital, and during this time I thought a lot about writing. I hadn't been able to write in about a month, the depression rendering me too numb to even try, to even pick up a notepad. My body and thoughts were pieces of wood too heavy to lift.

I had the hope that once my medication was stabilized, I would be able to write in the hospital. No distractions, no guilt, nobody needing me, no to-do lists. Absolutely none of the problems I spent scrutinizing in the first half of this essay. So, once I was feeling a little better and my moods were somewhat under control, I picked up my journal and waited for the words to come pouring out.

They didn't. They couldn't. While the new cocktail of medications prescribed by the hospital psychiatrist and doled out twice a day by the old man pushing the little metal cart was successful in erasing the violent mood swings, it was also successful in erasing *me*. My thoughts were garbled and unclear. I couldn't think of obvious, simple words that normally would have traveled from pen to paper without second thought. Words like "trouble" and "motivate." Ironically, one morning when I was trying yet again to get some thoughts down, it took me three whole minutes to think of the word "concentrate." And this wasn't just during writing, the same thing happened during conversation as well. The words just weren't there.

And they're still not. Which is why it was hard for me to come home and finish this essay. This essay that studies the act of writing through "physical surroundings" and "internal states." I am jealous of the woman who began writing this piece, who came up with these ideas, who had these kinds of problems. She took her gift for writing for granted. She thought she knew what it was like to "not be able to write." She didn't realize that the phrase "writer's block" at least still has something to do with being a writer.

I just spent about ten minutes rewriting each sentence in the above paragraph, not to ensure a smooth transition from one thought to the next, not in order to form crisp, direct sentences, certainly not to make sure I am drawing an accurate illustration of my feelings and ideas that will be clear to the reader. Those were my old reasons. The ones I took for granted—the type of editing a writer does. I spent ten minutes redoing the above paragraph (and this one) because it took that long for me to form sentences that I could follow; it took me that long to remember what I was trying to say from one sentence to the next.

So now the balancing act discussed in the earlier part of this essay has become more of a clear-cut choice. If I were single, if I didn't have children, would I flush these pills directly down the toilet? Absolutely. There is no question that these mood stabilizers are wreaking havoc on my creativity. In dulling the painful extremes of emotion, the medication is dulling my unique perspective of the world as well. And worse than that, dulling my ability to communicate that perspective to others. The mood stabilizers have simultaneously killed the one thing I most hate about myself, and the one thing I most cherish as well. I know other bipolar writers often refuse mood stabilizers for this very reason, and I wish more than anything I could join their ranks.

You can't strike a balance between opposites; no matter how hard a person tries, oil and water can't be mixed. So, for me, it's being a stable, nurturing mother and wife.

Though I still force myself to try to write, every day; I'm actually much more diligent about keeping a regular writing schedule than I used to be. But it's different now; it's more like physical therapy. I'm trying to keep my mind in as good a shape as possible. And when all else fails, I do crossword puzzles. Sometimes just connecting with words is a comfort.

If I didn't have Jon, Brooks, and Gabrielle, nothing would be more important than my writing. But if I didn't have them, nothing would be important. My children and my husband are my soul and my depth. Even when I am not directly writing about Jon's sense of humor, or Brooks' kindness, or Gabie's diva nature, they are always there, silently inspiring me and pushing the words along. They are everything I write and everything I want to write. So if the artist has to take a little break and let the mother have the space she needs to do her job well, the artist will do just that.

*   *   *

I have the sudden and immediate urge to go online and check my e-mail. I don't. I twirl my pen. I look around. I let out a long, slow breath, puffing out my cheeks. I twirl my pen. I twirl my hair. I look around. I remember I haven't talked to my mom in a while. I remember I'm fighting with my dad. There is still so much left to unpack. I need to schedule my appointment with the shrink. The kids' leftover Cheerios from this morning are cementing to the bowls. I have twenty-eight minutes! Think of how much I could get done!

I glance down at my watch on the table. Twenty-seven minutes. I pick up my notebook and hold it so close to my face it touches the tip of my nose. Nope. Still can't make anything useful out of any of it. I remember now that it was something about depression and motherhood, but that's it. All I can make out now is the half-finished sentence, *I'm someone that doesn't*, and next to it, *SHIT SHIT SHIT*.

I look at my watch. Twenty-six minutes. I stare at the blank page flickering at me from the laptop. Still a cliché. I type: Is there anything more humiliating than being a writer staring at a blank computer screen?

Back to the notebook, I tap a few ink-dot patterns onto the page before writing: It's weird that a person can feel selfish, guilty, unhappy, and nothing all at the same time. Shouldn't selfish negate guilty and unhappy? And surely the "nothing" should negate everything else. Bleah. That sounds weird. Weird and whiny. I'm coming across whiny. Maybe I'm not in the right frame of mind today. Maybe I'll wait until tomorrow . . .

No, I probably won't have a chance tomorrow. I know that. Twenty minutes.

I stand up and walk down the hall. I stretch. I stare at the blank wall and think about the family pictures that aren't hanging on it. I think of our five-year-old wedding pictures still tucked away in a box somewhere, loose, unframed. I've got to get going on that.

But not now. I walk back and forth a couple times and think about depression. How am I affected? How do I think other women are affected? How are families affected? How is my family affected? Am I selfish? Why did I scratch out my damn notes?

I'm thirsty. I head to the kitchen and get myself a glass of water. Wow, was I thirsty. I fill up again. The green glow of the microwave clock catches my eye. Fourteen minutes. I lean back on the counter and my arm hits a stack of bowls. I turn around and am confronted with this morning's fossilized Cheerios. Jon and the kids have been gone exactly twenty-one minutes, and I have exactly one full sentence—a sentence that sucks. I should have just done the damn dishes when I first had the thought, back when I still had twenty-eight minutes.

I force myself to take writing seriously, to insist on at least a few minutes a few times a week to work and send work out. I call myself a writer, even though secretly I fear I am a spoiled housewife with an expensive hobby. I try to think like an artist, but I'm not very good at it. Sometimes thinking like an artist feels diametrically opposed to thinking like a mother.

I'm beginning to see, though, that this lack of space has more to do with my internal state than it does my physical surroundings. There was no real reason I couldn't write when Jon took the kids to the park today. We live down the street from two coffee shops and a Denny's. And at work I have my own quiet office with a door and a lock and a computer that is far superior to my own.

My inner life is cramped and harried. My brain is a collage of unfinished to-do lists, phone numbers I'm supposed to remember, work files I forgot to bring home, grocery lists, involved ratios comparing my children's reading time vs. TV time, breakfast ideas, lunch ideas, dinner ideas, guilt, neuroses, things I didn't get done from the day before. I feel like there isn't any room inside for the writer I try to be, and somehow, I'm projecting that onto physical space. After four years of being a writer and a mother I'm so used to distractions that if none are present, I create them for myself.

I find it easiest to write in those unexpected bursts of ten-minutes of freedom, the beginning of *Sesame Street*, the time between the kids going to bed and Jon returning from work. But, while comfortable and easy, while fitting in with the rest of my spinning-out-of-control thought process, these stolen moments are hardly productive. They're rarely even coherent. And this attempt to appease the mother inside by reducing my writing down to an ignorable item on a perpetually ignored to-do list not only destroys my artistic productivity, it hurts my parenting as well.

Fourteen minutes.

I grab one more glass of water and head back to the dining room table. If I sit and write for fourteen minutes straight, without looking up, without thinking of anything else, I could probably get quite a bit done. Before I can write about this, I have to get past my guilt. I feel so selfish, so guilty. Is this even worth writing about? Maybe this doesn't deserve to be written. Maybe I don't deserve to write it.

I put the pen down and take a deep breath. I twirl my hair. Now I'm out of the essay and just jotting down random thoughts. I twirl my pen. I stand up and make one more sojourn down the hall. I think about the family pictures again. I think about a friend's wedding pictures, how much thinner I was in them than I am now. Thinking about that friend makes me think about cigarettes. Cigarettes! There are still a few left in the emergency-nervous-breakdown pack in my underwear drawer. I duck my head into the bathroom and check the blue plastic clock on the wall. Nine minutes left, plenty of time for a quick smoke.

A brief inventory of thirty-five minutes of writing: ten swear words, three or four scratched-out notes, six crossed-out sentences, three unfinished sentences, and five complete sentences.

Jon and the kids arrived home almost ten minutes early, just as I was reaching past a pile of bras and socks and grasping the pack of cigarette's crisp cellophane wrapper.

CHILDISH THINGS

LORI ROHLK PFEIFFER

MY HUSBAND gooses the red sports car we've rented for our European tour and it shoots over the hill like a little rocket. "See, it's fun to drive!" he says. "Don't you want to drive?" We are on our way to Brussels. It is the third day into our trip and I am unaccountably tired, like I have been up for weeks instead of merely a twelve-hour flight over the Atlantic Ocean. "No," I say, reclining the seat and pounding my jacket into a pillow. "I think I still have jet-lag."

I spend most of the two weeks we have in Europe suffering from jet-lag, and the two weeks after we get back to Arizona, too. But I have the final three chapters of my travel book to fact-check and edit and I am beginning to panic. The fatigue increases in intensity; I feel like I am slogging through a river with rocks in my pockets, like Virginia Woolf on a suicide mission. The water feels inviting. Or maybe I am Dorothy skipping through poisonous poppies on the way to Oz. Just a short nap, I think, just a snooze.

Then the puking begins. I can't believe I actually mistook being pregnant for endless jet-lag. I am now couch-bound, throwing up anything that passes my lips, anything that touches my lips, indeed, anything I think about. The baby inside me apparently isn't pleased with any earthly menu.

"You didn't do a very good job on these chapters." It is my husband, standing over me on the couch. The ceiling lights hurt my eyes. I feel both cranky and dreamy.

"If you don't like them, do them yourself," I croak, waving him away.

He does. He corresponds with my editor. He proofreads the maps and makes changes and sends everything off. I throw up until my ribs hurt and drag into the office a couple of times a week to look at my computer morosely before taking a pillow into the bathroom to sleep. I have plastic zip lock bags in the pockets of both my coats, in case I get up the energy to go someplace, like shopping or the bookstore, and can't get to the bathroom in time. But, increasingly, I don't go anywhere.

*   *   *

I quit my day job two years prior to write full time for magazines. I found my first assignment letter in the mailbox, for an article on job burnout, on my last day at work as a public relations director. I took it for a good omen.

I was well organized: I set goals, listed target magazines, made monthly and yearly plans and, of course, a five-year plan. I wanted to write a book before I was thirty-five. I didn't care what it was, as long as I was a published author. And then, I wanted to have kids.

It turns out I just made it in that order, a book and then a kid, just under my self-imposed deadline.

Uncharacteristically, the having kids part was rather vaguely thought through. Having had little experience with children, other than babysitting them occasionally, I imagined I would write up until the time I gave birth. After all, didn't Barbara Kingsolver write her first book when she was pregnant and struck with insomnia? I was looking forward to the insomnia. Then, I would put the baby within in arm's reach in a bouncy seat or cradle and write. The baby would entertain him or herself, first with a variety of baby toys like teething rings and beads, and then with books, small cars, building blocks, animals, and puzzles.

The extreme morning sickness makes it seem like the baby has other plans, but I'm in charge. I bounce from doctor to doctor looking for a way to stem the tide of nausea. I look like a poster child for starvation in a third-world country, gaunt cheeks, hollow eyes and ribs protruding over a tiny pot belly. One obstetrician tells me to enjoy my vacation. "I want to write," I protest, but no one hears me. My days are reduced to watching all three channels on our TV and crying a lot. I try to write, but my brain feels like a big fuzzy slipper. I turn down assignment after assignment. My belly grows, but the rest of me disappears.

*   *   *

The throwing up subsides a bit after I go to a high-risk specialist and start eating the same anti-nausea pills they give chemotherapy patients. But then they send me to get a heart test because of a murmur and I find out I have a fatal disease.

Suddenly, all of my hard work as a magazine writer doesn't seem important. The articles I published had a short shelf life, after all. Who will give a rip years from now whether or not I wrote a zippitty-do-dah article about glass blowing, international grocery stores, or Mexican pottery? My travel book seems pretty unimportant, too, and it hasn't even been printed. In fact, all of the writing in all the world's libraries seems insignificant when I think about dying.

I have primary pulmonary hypertension. The arteries in my lungs aren't elastic enough to oxygenate my body. The treatments are blood thinners and lung transplants. I could go within two years of diagnosis. A person with my condition isn't even supposed to be pregnant.

I correspond with some members of a group of people afflicted with PPH. One woman lives on a ranch in some Western state, more than an hour's drive from a doctor, longer from a hospital. She blew a hole in her heart giving birth. The baby is okay. She barely survived.

I think about the baby inside me not having a mother. I am beginning to feel like I know him. He tells me his name is Max—Maximilian August. He likes to swim inside me, like a little fish. He sticks his head, fists, and feet into my stomach, most days. Other times, he twirls around like a cat making itself comfortable on my lap. Only Max is inside.

In bed at night, we do Morse code on my stomach. Tap, tap, he goes, making rolling hills on my belly. Tap, tap, I respond, lightly drumming my fingers on his. We talk all the time. I tell him I'm sorry I am dying. I hope I can find him another mommy.

"Are you writing?" a friend asks.

"Yes," I lie. How can I explain that my brain feels all fuzzy like I'd been hitting the cold medicine really hard, and that writing doesn't seem to have any point anymore? I have been writing professionally for more than a decade. I have filing cabinets full of yellowed newspaper clippings. Who, besides my mother, reads them? I have just been killing trees.

I call people I haven't talked to in ages, friends or fellow writers, and update them on my life: I am pregnant and I am going to die.

The only friend my age who can talk about my impending death is my friend Deb. She talks with me for hours about how my husband would raise Max, though she doesn't think I need to find a substitute mom yet.

Deb, a writer too, is the only one not thrown by my other question: "What would you write if you only had a few months to live?"

I forget her answer, occupied with my own thoughts.

I try to free write, I go to poetry readings, I go to a psychiatrist, I write in long hand on a yellow notebook paper, I try to write late at night, I try to write lying in bed. I attempt different genres. Several short stories languish on my laptop. Essays sprout, but wither away.

What would you write if you only had a few months to live?

Would you write at all?

*   *   *

Max has been listening at the belly-button hole for nearly thirty-four weeks and now he's out in the world. The delivery was sudden—an unplanned birthday because Max was hanging around upside down in a nearly empty amniotic pool with the umbilical cord wrapped twice around his neck. The doctors were going to turn him today but I thought something was up and alerted the doctor. A quick ultra-sound and suddenly I find myself in the delivery room behind a curtain stretched across my chest. Minutes later I hear Max squeal. The cardiologist was there, but I didn't need him.

For the next few weeks, we fall into each other like lovers, cocooning against the troublesome, outside world. I cry every time I hear about a kidnapped or abused child on the evening's news. Finally, we get cable TV and I watch the listings channel slide by while he nurses, oddly comforted by a menu of what shows I could watch but choose not to.

And tomorrow morning I will turn on my computer. I do not today. Not most days. And when he naps I will type something up. Yes, maybe, well . . . no. I sleep with the baby. I feel very tired, still, and move as if I'm sleepwalking. My mind drifts while I endlessly change diapers and nurse him, milk dribbling down all my shirts, while I imagine that great throngs of cats will camp outside our door, drawn by the sweet-sour smell.

I dream about my writer self, but just can't get up the energy. I have friends who went back to work at six weeks after giving birth, but I am still hypnotized by the baby's smell. We stare at each other all the time, his eyes changing from dark slate to pool blue. I sing to him, even after he falls asleep.

Staying home and being a full-time mom is not easy. Seeing my name in print always gave me a little rush, like I was okay, like I'd done a good enough job to be printed. Getting paid for something I'd written made me feel validated. I felt like, with my name on a page someplace, I was somebody. Now, I feel like am merging with my baby, camping out in some unfamiliar territory, utterly lost. Hardly anyone tells me if I am doing a good job. Who knows yet?

*　　*　　*

One day, we are out for a stroll at the bookstore, when I spy a small blue journal. I had been feeling rather sad walking through the bookstore. Just a year-and-a-half earlier I had gone through the store with my husband and proudly noted that three of the magazines on the racks were carrying my stories. Now, I felt weirdly detached, as though I were walking through my old elementary school, amazed that nothing seemed to be quite the right size anymore. I wondered how I ever loved this place. It looked impossible now, all those books to be read, all those publications to write for.

But the journal gleams at me from the bookshelf, even though it is fashioned of suede leather and not at all shiny. It is tidily square and the color of a pastel Easter egg. A photo can be inserted in the small square cut-out in the front. Perfect.

I buy it and curl up on the couch during one of Max's naps, willing myself awake. I inscribe his name on the first page with hopeful script, then turn to page two and begin to write.

I want Max to know me, in case I am not be in his life. I want Max to understand how much I loved him, how much I pored over him during our first months together. I want what I write to make my son feel safe, to protect him from skinned knees and bullies and broken hearts, to tuck him in at night.

As I write in the journal I become drawn into the day-to-day details of caring for a baby. I record the way he sleeps (sometimes with his eyes open and smiling), and how his crying makes me feel helpless. How Vivaldi's "Four Seasons" soothes his colic. How, long before crawling, he managed to scoot sideways in crab fashion across the bed. How he turns into a happy, little boy.

The journaling seems sentimental to me. The entries would be about topics—childish topics—I would have scoffed at when I was younger and more ambitious, when I swore I would not be one of those older women in a poetry class writing about their children.

What I didn't understand then was that, as a mother, you lose the "I" voice and the perspective of a young, workaholic woman. Then, I wanted to be part of the world of money-making and prestige. I didn't value domestic life or children. Now, I seem drawn to less tangible ways of measuring worth. By recording my baby's life, my words take on a new cadence. I still feel like my life is ticking away, but my writing no longer matches that frantic speed. I write in long-hand, with a calligraphy pen and teal-blue ink. I feel like one of those Medieval monks, patiently copying sacred words onto a parchment that only a privileged few will read.

76

*   *   *

I have another appointment with a cardiologist, a new one. A second opinion, since the effects of pregnancy on my body have subsided. While the other cardiologist reminds me of Napoleon, standing there with his hand in his jacket and admonishing me "not to worry," the new one reminds me of Gandhi. He is peaceful. He is sensitive. His daughter has had leukemia. He is oh-so-sorry that I had to struggle through pregnancy with that awful diagnosis. That misdiagnosis.

I cry a lot now, but out of relief, not depression. I feel a reprieve. I rejoin the billions of people ignorant about the cause and timing of their impending deaths. It seems less likely my son will grow up motherless. I feel like everything is going to go back to normal, the way it was before I got pregnant.

But it doesn't. In between the baby and the disease, something has changed. Editors call me. I could write for them, but I take only a few assignments. I spend my days playing with my son. I dangle my feet in his plastic pool while he swims, scooting boats and fish back and forth. We stack wooden blocks and knock them down. We investigate ants and leaves and sticks in the back yard. I get down on my knees and growl like a bear. In public. We hang out with other mothers and their children and drink juice and complain about the Arizona heat.

"It's hot," I say, fanning myself.

"Yes," Max says. "Sun bright. Hot." Max drapes his long limbs over me, his blonde hair swirling down over his eyes and in ringlets just behind his ears. Everyone says he looks like an elf. "Mommy," he says, as if he is surprised to see me. He hugs me tight. "Hi Mommy. I love you, too!" Even though I haven't said anything.

*   *   *

Maybe I won't ever be able to go back to churning out magazine stories for money. I understand now that part of my brain is always distracted, always listening for my child.

Even when he is gone, with his father to the swimming pool, with our babysitter for a walk around the block, I listen for him. I cannot enjoy the small silences I have.

My ambition has been thwarted and softened. I realized I often brandished my words instead of used them, that being published made me feel accepted and important, that receiving a paycheck for something I created from scratch made me feel worthwhile.

Now my writing wanders where it will. Spending time with Max, immersing myself in toys and play and nature, makes me think of my own childhood. I write about growing up on a farm and see my mom and dad through a different perspective. I also write about my own development as a mother and a person. I have become more present-oriented; I sit still longer to see what wisdom emerges from my thoughts.

When I thumb through Max's journal and read the entries, I begin to see patterns and a slow succession of fits and starts and successes. Here he said his first sentence. There he learned to walk up stairs. He smiles all the time. He likes books and pretty flowers and bees. Maybe I am being a good mom after all. The terrible twos seemed to blossom early and fade quickly. Most of the entries I write are positive; my fears and ineptitudes fade as well.

This year, shortly after Max turns two, I fill up the last pages in his little blue journal. Then I pick up a new journal, the exact same kind, but in a slightly darker shade of blue, and begin writing again. It becomes clear that I am writing not only about him, but what currently is my life's work, these childish things.

THANKS, MOM

KATHERINE ARNOLDI

80

A FIRE WELL KEPT

KATIE KAPUT

"YOU WANT TO HAVE A BABY?" She was one in a constant stream of friends confused as heck by a transsexual dyke like myself wanting a baby, especially with a partner whose gender changed with the tides.

"Won't it distract you from what you really want to do with your life?" No one seemed to understand that having a loving, creative home and family life was a crucial part of what I wanted to do with my life: create writing and art from a space that felt real and healthy to me.

"How will you find time to write? Or do anything?" I was grinding my teeth before I heard this; after she said it, I crushed my teeth to dust.

Talking on the phone with friends from back home had become really frustrating as soon as Ricky and I decided to have a baby. Everyone thought eighteen was much too young to even think about having children.

"We'll make time. It'll be okay. And think of all the new stuff I'll have to write about!" I believed what I was saying, but I couldn't help being scared. What if having a baby smothered whatever imaginative spark I had? What if I got so wrapped up in the baby that I forgot I wanted to write?

I decided to spare myself any further need to justify my decision. "I've gotta go."

It was so hard not to get wrapped up in the nets everyone kept throwing at us, trying to hold us in the past. It was hard to believe that people who had been wise about so many things in the past could be so totally wrong all of a sudden. It's tough not to doubt yourself in the silence left behind when you hang up the phone on old friends questioning your right to be a dynamic, changing person.

I surveyed the apartment I had been sharing with Ricky for less than six months, an admittedly short time in which to decide to have a child with someone. But I wanted to have a baby every time I looked at the space we had made. The dried roses, her apron hanging in the kitchen, her paintings piling up in the bedroom—all of it felt right.

We had been trying to get pregnant since we moved in together. There was a sense of urgency, even though we were both just approaching twenty. I might never be able to get her pregnant in the future because I was taking estrogen, and she might never want to be pregnant again, since she wanted to take testosterone.

We had to be ready. The three years we had been in love with each other seemed too long not to seize this opportunity; we had wanted children too long to lose this one chance at being the kind of family we dreamed of being.

We were creative people—making art, a home, a baby, a family. I searched for what strength I would have left and pledged it to my writing.

I would have my partner, my child, and my art.

I put water on for pasta in the little black pot; I sang for an audience of one: whatever grrrliespermie might meet herself a gentleman egg tonight. I hoped she would use her spark to start a fire, filling our lives with warmth.

*   *   *

And when the grrrliespermie met the gentleman egg, the most fantastic thing happened.

His name would be Rio Francesco. As a fetus, his name was Cuddles. In his ultrasound photos, he looked right at us and made a funny little metalhead face—little baby Eddie the Iron Maiden skeleton. Perhaps we had a budding musician coming into our lives? At least we knew he had good taste in music, and a hell of a sense of humor.

I used my writing to get all my hopes out into the world, the way I couldn't wait for Cuddles to come out and hope his own hopes.

I wrote about the waiting, the making, and the dreaming. I wrote about talking with Ricky about making a baby, months before we moved in together, sitting on springtime swings in the nighttime park by my parents' old house. I tried to capture with words the way Ricky looked, kicking her feet on that swing, just like I imagined our kid doing someday, kicking his way around inside of Ricky or dangling his feet off of his own swing, begging to be pushed higher like Ricky did as a kid, or whining to be left alone to sway in the wind the way I did, little sissy that I was.

There had never been anything more inspiring than our fetus working on becoming a real live baby. My head was full of starry possibilities. My dreams were full of kids of all ages doing all sorts of things with me. I danced with them. I tucked them into bed. I read them books: ones I loved or hated as a child, ones I wrote, and even ones they wrote themselves.

*   *   *

The last few weeks of the pregnancy were nearly sleepless. Ricky was miserable. She hated being pregnant; it ran counter to everything she wanted from her body. She was embarrassed and upset by her chest.

I started going with her to school, both to keep her from feeling like a hideous freak, and to be there in case there were any baby-related emergencies. We were both anxious for the baby to get his butt into the outside world. It seemed like it might happen at any moment. I certainly didn't want to be unavailable for the few hours of school Ricky had every couple of days. We wanted to be together for the whole experience. I knew I would regret it forever if I weren't there to help her when she went into labor.

The sleep deprivation made everything hilarious, astonishing, upsetting. We laughed about what we might call all those interesting body parts around the baby: winky, tinky, hickorydickorydock, and all that jazz. We watched endless children's movies, and wept at all the sad parts that had so affected us as kids. I had the most vivid dreams about my son—his life, his voice, his cry, all in blazing Technicolor at a midnight movie back home in Chicago.

How could I write about any of this? There was no way to translate it into words at the time. I knew I would never have another chance to write down my feelings as they were, but there was no language for my fears and hopes. How do you adequately articulate the feeling of your life ending and being replaced by something new and fuller? How do you sequentially tell the story of a big old bang sending a new life expanding in all directions for what you hope will be eternity? You can't be in all places at once, you can't tell all sides of any one story, and there are certain moments when the enormity of everything a person can experience in nine months overwhelm any hope of expression. I decided to leave off my resistance and enjoy the ride, instead.

My personal creativity felt impossibly smaller than the creativity of life itself, and infinitely more worthwhile than at any other time in my life.

* * *

Ricky's prelabor lasted for days. At three in the morning on the twelfth of June, the pace of her labor quickened. In the hospital, I shut out as much of my own worries and excitement as possible to focus on her. I didn't shave. I didn't brush my teeth or eat. I felt like I was running around the room taking care of her every whim, but I know I mostly just held her hand and whispered reassurances and encouragements to her. I felt nearly powerless; I had an urge to do something. I did everything I could think of to help her, which mostly consisted of doing what she said.

There was far more blood than I had ever seen come from one person, and much more moaning. Ricky was braver and tougher than I could dream of being, although I would love a chance to try.

Rio came out, ending up in my arms. Ricky didn't want to hold the baby right away; she was in too much pain. I think she also knew I was worried about creating a bond with Rio, since I had always longed to give birth to my child myself.

After the birth, existence shrank to include only my partner, my son, and I. The midwife disappeared, Ricky's family went blurry, and the friends calling on the phone became background noise.

I had so much to say to these two people, the most important people in my life, yet I felt I had no need to say it. I smiled at Rio, I kissed Ricky, and I let my tears flow.

It was like losing touch with the world while creating my own with words, only this time I believed the rest of the world was never coming back. Sometimes I think it still hasn't, and never will.

*   *   *

For the first four months of Rio's life, watching him sleep, eat, and grow kept me satisfied (not to mention busy) enough with my life that I didn't think much about writing. When he started playing by himself some of the time, I remembered I was truly separate from him. I remembered I had creative urges with which I needed to reconnect. I felt a sense of loss at not having done more writing before having Rio. Not because I wished I had waited to have him, but because had I used and appreciated my time as well before having a son as after, I would have a pile of completed (perhaps even published) manuscripts to my name.

I used every scrap of time I didn't need for Rio or my relationship with Ricky to handwrite a series of fictional diaries, released as zines, about a transsexual girl finding her place in the world, the way I had found mine after so much struggle. Sometimes my partner watched the baby while I wrote; other times I kept an eye on his attempts to swallow his rattle whole, constantly talking to him and scribbling out my story, complete with illustrations.

Ricky started painting again, and did some writing of her own. Raising a child with someone who understands the need for self-expression made all the difference. We made sure there was plenty of time for both of our imaginations to find nourishment. We took turns. We found that we were more productive making art since becoming parents. We had more energy, more focus, and more appreciation for how precious and fleeting time, energy, and inspirational experiences are.

I was right and wrong about everything. I couldn't find time to write; we had to make it. I didn't just have new things to write about; I had lost old things. I set things aside to become a mama to the most astonishing person I had ever met. I picked up new things when I got the chance; Rio gave me more and more things as he explored the world. He brought me treasures from places I had never been, took me on adventures of which I could never have dreamed before him.

Ricky and I may have sparked a whole new fire, but we have also kept our own fires burning.

85

OUR (Publishing) HOUSE

GAYLE BRANDEIS

WHEN I found out that my first book, *Fruitflesh: Seeds of Inspiration for Women Who Write*, was going to be published, I lost it. I sobbed, I blubbered, I laughed hysterically, I spewed snot all over my face. Years of work, years of waiting for this news, had finally come to fruition, and I almost couldn't handle it. I felt like I was going to burst out of my skin. I was over the moon. Then I went to pick up my kids at school. As soon as they got in the car, I turned to them, my face still all streaky, and said, "Guess what? I just sold my book!" They looked at me for about a second, and said, "That's cool." Then they immediately started to fight over a cache of lychee gel snacks, and I plummeted right back down to earth (which, all in all, is not a bad place to be.) Kids definitely keep a published mama grounded.

They keep a briefly-in-the-spotlight mama grounded, too. At my first *Fruitflesh* event (the event where my wrap shirt unwrapped and I ended up sharing a lot more of my own fruitflesh than I had planned), my eight-year-old daughter kept my book-signing chair warm while I read. Later, as I was signing books, she sat next to me and signed people's cocktail napkins. At a different reading, during the Q&A session, she asked me to dance (I did a little spin to humor her.) At one of the first readings for my novel, *The Book of Dead Birds*, the following year, my twelve-year-old son lay on the floor of the bookstore, right near the stage, like he was the victim at a crime scene waiting to be traced in chalk.

This, as you may imagine, was very distracting. A while later, after he popped back up, he and his sister discovered the rocking chair in the aisle of books that happened to be in my peripheral vision. They began rocking each other back and forth maniacally, laughing under their breath. I had to stop reading, turn to them, and say, "Please don't make me be a mom right now." It got a laugh, but it also made me fume. It didn't seem fair that in my moment of glory, I had to deal with their ridiculousness. It was hard to fully focus on the page after I started to read again. When my book tour took me out of town, I was grateful for the break.

I am not the kind of person who craves attention, but it's nice not having to share that small pool of light while I am on the road. It's nice to be able to talk to other grown-ups about the creative process without having someone blow a straw wrapper at my face. It's nice to be able to eat room service banana cream pie in a bed whose sheets I don't have to wash (not that I wash ours all that often). It's nice that my husband's job lets him telecommute so he can be home with the kids while I travel. It's nice to talk to my sweet people on my cell phone each night before I burrow under those clean (not to mention insanely high thread count) sheets and dream my very own dreams. It's nice that when I wake up, the only person I have to worry about getting ready is me. It's nice to come home and remember that's where I really belong.

My writing life and my mothering life are so intertwined; each one provides an escape from the other, but each one helps me enter the other more deeply, too. Most of the time, they braid together fairly seamlessly, but there have been a few kinks. Ever since I made the leap from writer to "author," my son won't let me look at his writing. He has no problems with me looking at his geometry homework, or at the maps he draws for world history, but he won't let me look at the papers he writes for language arts, and grudgingly lets me glance at the reading summary I have to put my signature next to every day. I promise him that I won't judge his work harshly, that I won't ever put the kind of expectations on his writing that I do on my own, but he still won't let me near his words. It makes me sad that he feels compelled to do this, especially since I know the written word is something that can connect us—my daughter loves to write and I love sharing in her writing—but I have to honor his desire for privacy.

I understand that desire; most of the time I keep my own writing private, tucked away from my kids. They see me writing all the time, but they don't often see what I write. If I felt like they were looking over my shoulder, it would stifle me and my process. I try to write as if they're never going to read my work. I try to write as honestly and as freely as I can, and sometimes that takes me to some very un-kid-friendly places. So when they both asked to read *The Book of Dead Birds* after it was published, I was hesitant. The story covers some pretty dark and disturbing, not to mention adult, stuff—prostitution, lots of stinky dying birds, a dose of Ecstasy—and I didn't want to freak them out. I almost asked them to wait until they were older, to be content just reading their names in the acknowledgements section for the time being, but I had recently written an anti-censorship essay and wanted to practice what I had just preached.

"Some of this might be painful to read," I warned them. "If you have any questions about anything that happens in the book, just let me know." They solemnly agreed. My daughter read the book first. I watched her face as she turned the pages—sometimes concerned, sometimes delighted, always absorbed. When she finished, I asked if she was okay.

"I loved it," she told me, beaming with pride. My sweet girl. I asked if anything in the book upset her; she said that when she came to a section that she knew was going to be difficult, she just skipped over it. Then she went into her room, and, much to my surprise, created a board game based upon the book. She made a whole pile of cards with trivia questions about the story (a sample: "True or False: Helen's best friend was Moon." Flip the card over: "False, her name was Sun.") She made a twisty-turny path on the board you would advance or fall back on depending on whether or not you got the question right. The game pieces were pennies. She had obviously read the book carefully. And understood it. And created something of her own out of it. I was blown away; that meant more to me than any good review ever could.

My son liked the book, too, but he was a little weirded out. Not really by the book itself, he told me, but by the fact that I had been thinking about the things in the book. I guess it would be weird to realize that your mom has been living in a world of GI bars and bird incinerators at the same time that she's been making your peanut butter sandwiches and driving your car pool. To realize that your mom has been living a double life, a shadow life, without ever leaving the house. To realize that she wouldn't have it any other way.

I am enamored of the birth metaphor when it comes to the creative process: you conceive of a story, a poem, a piece of art; you let it gestate, you let it grow and kick inside you; you birth it into the world, still dripping with the waters of your inner-life. Getting published doesn't quite fit that metaphor, but it still seems very mama-centric, just situated a few years after the birth. For me, having a book published, once I got over the initial hysteria, felt like taking my son to school for the very first time.

On that day I held his hand as we walked across the street. I gave him a hug inside the classroom, but then I had to let him go; I had to leave him there. It was a lot harder for me than it was for him—he was excited to be around new toys, new kids, the smell of new crayons, but I felt bereft. My body was used to having him around; my eyes were used to tracking his every move. I spent the day crying, wondering if he would make friends, if he would get bullied, if his teacher would appreciate him. Sending my first book out into the world was a similar feeling—will people like it? Will critics be bullies? Will the world embrace this word-child of mine? So much of parenting, so much of publishing, is about letting go, often resisting it, but realizing it is necessary. And, ultimately, it is good.

When it was time for my daughter to start school, it was a little easier; I had already gone through the experience once. Same with having a second book published—I knew more about what to expect. That didn't erase all my fears, though; I still fretted over whether my girl would be happy, whether my characters would find acceptance in the world. I knew that all I could do was stand at the fence and leak tears and blow kisses and watch them disappear around the corner. And then I went home, my heart aching with love, and I set upon creating something new.

PALMA SOLEADO

ROSANA CRUZ

MY FIRST gig back was a cush one—outdoors on a sunny New Orleans day in a shady cobblestone courtyard with a curlicued iron gate. We played a small party for the Latin American Studies department at one of the universities. Our band's repertoire of traditional Cuban "folk" music from the 20s and 30s, called Son, would fit right in with the sun dappled, almost rustic surroundings. It was an afternoon lit by the yellow-green tints and flowery pinks of spring. Birds were chirping as I approached the microphone. My bandmates started playing and I broke out on cue—

"*Me fui a Palma Soleado...*"

The heavy, breathy outburst, loud for effect, was such an amazing release. It seemed to pull itself up from the very bottom of my guts, damp and pungent like the humidity in the tiny Cuban town I was singing about. The notes thumped and thudded inside of me, reverberating between the roof of my mouth and my nostrils, a part of my body I only learned about when I started singing. I relished that gig, the perfect setting for songs about trees and spiders and whole farms burning down, everyone coming together to rebuild them. It was warm and early and people were taking a break from working, the music a welcome, if unusual, interruption. The crowd was ideal for a gentle return to the stage. I could sing my rusty old heart out, my four month old son, Rey, snuggled against me, sometimes nursing, in his sling.

My last gig before my pregnancy hiatus had been about six months earlier, a holiday show at a club downtown where we redid Christmas carols and Hannukah songs into danzones, guarachas, and cha cha chas. I was so big people couldn't believe I had another two months to go in the pregnancy. I only took the stage for a few songs and then danced with friends the rest of the time. At one point I had to sit at the bar to catch my breath and, taking advantage of my stillness, the baby started kicking. At first I laughed, and then my jaw dropped and I drew my friend's hand to my belly so she could share my disbelief. The kid was kicking out the rhythm of the cha cha cha the band was playing. I was floored. In that moment, in my body, my creative life was merging with a life I was helping create. My heart felt like it was about to burst out of my body; the thrill of two merging loves, my baby-to-be and my music, overwhelmed me.

90

Being pregnant was like carrying around my own little muse. The connections between being pregnant and being creative seemed so obvious, so monstrously real and in my face. The signs were like anvils falling from the sky, big and immediate against random little doubts that crept up in passing conversations that I, once in a while, fretted over. "I guess you won't be hanging out in smoky bars much anymore, huh?" "It was nice while it lasted, but I bet you won't want to give up sleep just to gig." "You're really gonna keep singing after the baby? You say that now but . . ." But the energy that was coming out of me at the time was too much not to sing. Or write. Everything elicited some type of creative urge, a desperate and joyful need to document and interpret. It was the storyteller inside of me with some great material and a captive audience. And for me, my belly housed the most perfect audience, the one who pushed me to be truthful (he was so close, I couldn't lie) and inspired me to say it and sing it as beautifully as I felt it.

I had wanted to both write and sing from the time I was very young, but I think lots of folks experience what I did—you get shamed out of singing. It becomes something that creates a division between those who have "talent" and the rest of us. This set-up pushed me to write privately and to explore visual arts, partly because I figured I could always just hide them or easily excuse them away by saying I hadn't finished them yet. I was defending myself from too much as an adolescent to be vulnerable to criticism for singing, making myself heard, enjoying my voice. Even in college the pecking order dogged me among honey-voiced girls with guitars. Eventually, I let "them" win and abandoned any musical interests to my bass playing girlfriend who sang in choir all through childhood and was classically trained.

When I finally became a singer, in my late twenties and almost by accident, it was only because I was given a chance to sing traditional Cuban music that I dared to take the stage. A local musician needed a babysitter so that he could go into the studio during the day. I babysat his daughter, and later attended some of his shows. We became friends. One day he asked me if I knew anyone who could sing, that he was thinking about starting a Cuban band. I was shameless, inviting myself into the band. I told him I didn't know if I could sing, but that I loved the music and that I would give it my best. It was terrifying. I can't even remember my first gig. But the songs, I remember the songs. Early in the band's history we busked on the street, feeling tentative until we actually got going. As my voice bounced off the old buildings around us, the rich, hollow thud of the bongos and the clanga-twang of the tres guitar wove around and up and down. I saw the prized roosters and felt the abyss of heartbreak that we sang about and I was mystified by people who managed to walk right past us and not even notice. For me, the street had been transformed.

When I sang "Mango Mangue," a song extolling the fruits of my home island, my stomach would fill with butterflies and I could feel my heart beating in my chest, like it wanted to leap out and fly to where I always want to be. The power the music had over me, conjuring memories of my grandfather listening to his Barbarito Diez records, of my mom dancing in her chancletas, her flip-flops, in the kitchen, of long rides on dusty country roads as I prayed for time to stop—this music pushed me to be brave. I wanted it to sound good, sure, but more than that I needed to sing this stuff. I needed to go back to those places. I needed to access that creative connection with where I came from. It was through this band that I met and fell in love with the man that I now affectionately call "my baby daddy." Through this band, through becoming a singer, I became a mother.

And yet it hasn't all been flowing poetry and free babysitting. It kicks my ass, constantly challenging, constantly pushing, constantly making me fight and negotiate in turns to remind myself and the world that I am both mother and singer. While that first day back was smooth, the late night gigs were harder to get back to. I would be tired and forget lyrics. My big mama body felt awkward in my tighter-than-before stage clothes, my front woman bravado was harder to come by when my brain was foggy and my breasts were full of milk. One time when I had an early evening gig, I had my neighbor bring the baby to the bar and hang out with him while I sang. The bartender got twitchy about some permit or law or something and made them leave. They stood outside and watched me through the glass and I felt split, but I kept singing. Just past my reflection I saw my son's face. It showed his awe and joy and longing and, immediately, my voice was filled with it. It was one of our best shows ever. We joked that it was a shame he was too small to carry the tip bucket around himself.

I've learned more about fun and good feeling in the past three years than I did in all of the getting high and getting naked of my twenties. The kid has music spilling all over him constantly. His dad hauls the big upright bass to at least four gigs a week. Sometimes Rey is cutting-up right in front of the stage. There are brass bands in the streets and jazz performers on the corners. We clean to loud, cheesy pop music (when Papi, the music snob, isn't home) and blast The Ramones just for fun and joy-crazy dancing. Friday evening happy hours happen in the enormous fenced-in yard of a local bar with little kids weaving through the tall grasses just a few feet from the featured band. Again and again we participate in that delicious ritual, a pure connection of music to ear to heart, pumping through the body then back to the musician. I know he got that from us, but he gives it right back. I don't think I can ever reproduce the voice I sang in, standing at the microphone, my child feeding at my breast. Now he comes to band practice and tries to take over. He wants to play all the instruments and is our harshest critic; he actually heckles us, yelling, "Stop! Stop singing that SONG!"

Eventually the creativity/mama anvils were becoming light and transparent. I felt a well of music building up and then my friend Morgan died, the person who, way back when, helped to remind me that actually, I *did* love country music. Once night I had a gig with the Son band, but I wasn't really feeling it. For all the misery and pain that can be encompassed in our music, in Son music it didn't feel right in my skin. My mind kept wandering back to a Freakwater song—the first Morgan ever played for me. The "Waitress Song"; it was fitting for her. Not just because she waited tables, but because she had that sardonic, snappy wit in her tableside comebacks. We took a set break and I felt a chill as I remembered Morgan's last visit here and how we had walked down this same street, stopping to hear brief slices of music in front of this bar or that. I took the stage and said a few words about my friend who'd been killed that week in a car wreck. Then I just started singing, quavering voice and all. I just kept on, singing out all the irony, all the twisted together pleasure and hurt that I felt right then. That night, some friends and I started what we call our "pirate dub country band." And Rey's presence remains solid in my musical life. He loves country music as much as I do. My kid forces me to practice by demanding that I sing songs that I worry, slightly, are a bit much for his young, cheery disposition; "Don't Wake Me 'til Its Over," "It Wasn't God Who Made Honky Tonk Angels," "I Can't Keep My Hands Off You," "Jesus Doesn't Want Me for a Sunbeam." Aside from Rey's encouragement, this material is good too; it keeps me honest. Roots music, right? Music about dirt and pain and beauty, it can't be sung without feeling.

I know I think too much on stage. I lose focus. I feel amped and nervous and I can't stay present. I have less air, and struggle on the lower notes. There are things that I edit right after they come out. I think about what was still too low, about the mic and whether I should use it or not, whether I'm keying and hitting and smooth, or if I was rough in the wrong ways. Being up there is so immediate it can overwhelm me, make me scramble through and want to hide. I get scared. I can't connect to the audience. I have to work to get to that place where I remember, "Hey, this is sacred. This is magic and pure and it's okay, let it go, let it happen. The love is the sound. They give it and you send it back. Don't be shy or hide or play it off. Don't do things out of a place of fear." The place of love and strength and the divine, this is the place where my voice lives. I have to let go of the thinking and just feel. I have to be present with my feelings, just like I have to do with my kid. Sneaky parenting tactics never work for us, we just have to struggle through and appreciate that, in the end, at least we were real.

Our first live show with the country band was beyond real, it was surreal. We played a tiny dive bar that seemed like a cross between a church and a barn. There was a dog and a bunch of cab drivers and maybe ten other people. I suited up in my country-punk armor and took the stage like I hadn't in years. I didn't need a mic. I bellowed and I crooned, all me, my voice stripped bare but steady, flowing into the half-empty bar. My son, sitting with my friends, grinned back at me, and together we filled the room.

92

CROWNING

JACEY BOGGS

IN THE dilapidated neighborhood of my childhood, you could reach out your kitchen window and touch the peeling paint on the house next door. Good kids ran the streets only until the streetlamps came on; dogs were for protection instead of companionship; and girls needed only to look good, lie down, and have babies. I was taught to think of myself more or less in these terms. The idea that I aspired to grow up, move away, and have a career, was revolutionary. That my career would be as an artist was unimaginable.

There was only room for one artist in my loving but dysfunctional family, and that was my brother, Matt. He was seven years my senior and he could draw anything. Stick it in front of him and he could reproduce it. This was art in the poor northeast Kansas City neighborhood that fomented my person the first fifteen years of my life. There was no abstract interpret me art, no soft lines or blurred colors, no passionate release or deep message. Nope—a watercolor of a shoe, a pen drawing of your mom, a colored pencil sketch of a pelican on a pier, or an excruciatingly detailed and armed comic book, that was real art. That was real potential. That was something I couldn't do, potential I didn't have. My brother had the world spread out before him.

I went to school and got straight A's. I studied and stayed up until early morning reading in my closet. I was not an artist. I was the smart and good daughter, the kind that wasn't even supposed to want to be an artist. At times I boasted that I'd be a lawyer, even though I hadn't the foggiest idea what a lawyer did. I only knew they didn't live in northeast Kansas City, and eat macaroni and cheese with peas and canned tomatoes for dinner—at least they didn't on TV. My mother vehemently thought I should be an airline stewardess. "All that glamour and travel," she'd exclaim. "You'd look adorable in those little dresses!" I figured I'd end up a teacher—noble, struggling, and sadly underappreciated. Sometimes, though, I'd admit that what I really wanted to be was an artist. I wanted to be expressive and tragic. I ached to be inspired and confident enough to let what was inside of me color what was outside of me. I longed to have an inside that was colorful enough to need to come out.

94

A decade or so later, twenty-five years old and five months pregnant, I made Ol' Crazy Pete. At the time, my belly barely rounded, but I wrapped my arm around it like it was the weight, or the jewel, of the world. My partner was out of town for the weekend and I was feeling alone, a bit co-dependently lost, and bored when I noticed, for the gazillionth time, that the bathroom door was held open by a rusty pair of needle nose pliers wedged between it and the floor. This makeshift doorstop was put in place to keep the out-of-plumb door from swinging open and settling somewhere around the middle of its trajectory. Aside from shakily and unattractively doing its job, it had gouged a hole in the already dingy linoleum. I decided, in all my pregnant glory, to do something about it. With that decision I became a woodworker.

Ol' Crazy Pete was what I named the piece I made that day, although I wasn't calling them pieces yet (that came after the word artist, when used to refer to me, stopped making me bristle). He was a wooden wedge about five inches long with a spiky, red-haired head cut into the non-tapering end so that, when placed under the door, you could see the two faces, one coming and the other going. I made it out of an old piece of two-by-four stud that I found in the garage, nothing fancy. I carefully cut it with a jigsaw (after I figured out how to use it), sanded it by hand, and painted it with acrylic paint. Since I was still operating under the illusion that I was not an artist and couldn't do artistic things, I didn't think I could draw eyes. Instead, I painted red and blue spirals where eyes would normally be. These cartoonish symbols for crazy were what inspired title.

It didn't feel like art, it felt like some home improvement project. I wasn't creating, I was stretching my new homeowner muscles. This is what made it possible and not too intimidating to attempt. In the end, I definitely felt accomplished, but not necessarily artistic.

By the end of that week, I had made five more doorstops. By the end of the month, fifteen—plus I had started carving tiny features in their faces. I started to feel a bit more confident, artistic, and creative. I decided to call myself CarveGirl, build a website, and start selling doorstops. However, after the first forty doorstops, I never wanted to look at a doorstop again, much less make one. I moved on to bookends and light-switch plates. From there, on to kids toys, mirrors, and tables, learning as I went and loving every new project. With each bit of woodworking I did, a little bit more of the artist hiding inside me came out. Had I not been pregnant, my artistic side would have been forever confined to wistful, rainy-day musings done mostly while staring out of trendy coffee shop windows, furtively glancing at hip art students with paint and plaster on their worn dickies.

I reveled in this new creative energy. My body was carrying a tiny fetus, and I carried that thought around with me like I carried the new and tiny weight in my uterus. As I swelled heavier and heavier, so did the feeling. I was creating something from nothing. A little, perfect person was growing inside me where a little person had not been before. The idea that I was already a creator by makeup, that it was an inherent ability, must have nested in my brain. It gave me confidence. I started to think more and more of what I could do in this world. A catch-22, I know: because I'm a girl, all my life I was systematically led to, and forced to drink from, the stream of *You're good at looking good and having babies*; but because I'm a girl and because I had that baby, I found that I'm much more than that. I'm a woman capable of creation.

Pregnancy and childbirth changed me immensely and irreversibly. Most mind-blowingly, it gave me the most scrumptious little nugget of a boy to watch over until he can do so himself. It showed me an interior I had long forgotten and never properly explored. It gave me feminism—a fire inside. It gave me confidence. My body's natural ability to get pregnant and create a warm, safe home for a growing life, made me accept that other abilities exist inside me. I gained a clear sense that I was capable of doing whatever I wanted to do; I could be what I'd always longed to be. Pregnancy made me an artist.

Everything I create is heavily and directly influenced by the fact that this is the world that my son lives in. I want to change it into a kinder, more compassionate world where he doesn't have to subjugate women and people of color to avoid being ostracized by society or make his own life seem more meaningful; where he isn't trapped by anybody else's vision of what he should be; where he isn't expected to hide his emotions and he's free to seize, without fear, any and all of the love that he has heart enough to feel; where he can embrace and celebrate differences, instead of being afraid of them or pretending they don't exist or matter, and know that humanity is not a liability, but something people actively strive for.

This is the world I'm trying to help create with everything I make. In the window-gazing daydreams of my high school career, I pictured myself as a dark and tortured artist, scouring my pain-blackened soul and scratching my art out of the harshest aspects of my black-clad life. However, now that I am an artist, that description couldn't be further from the truth. I'm a smart, creative, funky, lactating woman, hair shimmering with the lathe's chunky sawdust and a toddler's peach pit in my pocket because I'm too busy to make the trek into the kitchen to throw it away. I'm a smiling girl. Even when I deal with the shittier aspects of life, the parts I'm unsatisfied with—and being a vegan, anarchist punk-rocker living in America, there are many things that I find wholly unsatisfying—I try to reflect more on what it could or should be, than what it is. This is a trait I hope to instill in my son—the talent of seeing shabby things and trying to change them, rather than seeing shabby things and letting them change you.

Changing the world is what I hope to do, and what I hope my son will strive to do. I'm not naïve enough to think that we will immediately effect grand, land-sweeping change, but hopefully I'll never be jaded enough to stop trying. It's the trying that makes our lives worth something.

Perhaps it's because of my youth spent as an ornamental, strictly-there-as-scenery girl, too often relegated to the sidelines, believing that I didn't have the power to do any-

95

thing worthwhile so I might as well just look pretty, hold the important people's jackets and watch things unfold, but creating utilitarian things is incredibly fulfilling for me.

It's so satisfying to make something that I know will be used in a very real and everyday way—tables, chairs, mirrors, perpetual calendars, bookcases, toys, chalkboards, light switch plates. I cut, carve, and paint them with their use and users in my mind. It's secondary that they are (hopefully) interesting, pretty, and impart a message. I'm doing something, so is my art, and whether my son decides to be a painter, sculpture, furniture maker, musician, or something entirely different and/or non-artistic, I hope that he never falls for that sticking-yourself-on-the-sidelines trap. Life's too short and too full of possibility to not *do* something or *make* something.

The thought that I am an artist, that I actually make things that function as they are intended, that people use, need even, is often louder than the table saw's whirling, twirling, toothy grin. From the start of the process to the end, it feels like art. Every stage of the process, from the idea to the sketchbook to the woodshop to the painting, feels creative. When I'm doing it, each part feels like my favorite (except the sanding, jeez that takes forever!). Four days a week I nurse my twenty-month-old and then I make my way to the woodshop. It strikes me on those days just how far I've come from that shabby neighborhood where I grew up. Whenever I forget it and think, "I can't possibly be an artist!" all I have to do is look at my portfolio and, even more so, my son, and know the girl who can't do anything but look good, lie down, and have babies is a figment, a lie. Then I shake off the insecurity and go back to subverting the dominant paradigm one power tool at a time.

ON THE ROAD WITH DANGERBABY

JEN THORPE

MY LIFE is a work in progress.

Well, whose life isn't really? That's just such a great opening line. Of course, it's probably been used before, but I'm too tired to check. I may be directly plagiarizing somebody, but I'm too tired too check, too tired to care. These are the things that define my life now; constant fatigue, a devil-may-care attitude towards most things which don't concern the care of a two-year-old, extreme patience interspersed with moments of transcendental joy and mind numbing frustration.

My son, Samwise Danger Thorpe, was born September 1, 2001. He is two-years-old. I'm watching him now as he plays by the window with a little toy mouse. He's wearing clothes made entirely by myself, a pink and red candy-striped skirt (made the morning of the Pride Parade to help blur some gender lines) and a T-shirt that I screen-printed with my own design of two kids in silhouette, sporting mohawks. Sure he *looks* cool, but what about his quality of life? At least I can say that he's well traveled, in fact Sam is a seasoned tour baby. He has been on tour through the western U.S., around Europe, and by the time you read this he'll have done the eastern states too.

I am the singer in a ten-year-old d.i.y. punk band called Submission Hold and Sam's dad, Andy, is the bass player. Two of Sam's first words were "bass" and "mo" (Samspeak for music). In utero he was at a show we played in front of three thousand kids in a hockey arena (they weren't there just for us, the headliners were a much loved indie band from DC).

All kids love music, but I like to think Sam has a genetic predisposition toward it. He loves to sing, dance, and play with any and all musical instruments. And he is good at touring. A natural. His first tour was early in the summer of 2002, when he learned to crawl. Before that tour we were a bit nervous. Sure, we'd seen crazy things on the road, but tossing an eight-month-old baby into the van seemed the height of insanity. As it turned out, our worries were all for naught—this was the best tour that I'd ever been a part of, due in no small part to Sam's presence. Coupling my old true love of life on the road with my newfound love of Sam was truly a winning combination.

The scene in which we live, play, and travel was and is beyond supportive. For the most part, people were very eager to provide Sam and us parents clean, quiet spaces to retreat to. Of course there were some European squats which were so filthy that I'd never dream of putting my still-crawling babe on their floors. Particularly one squat in Belgium. The venue was in an old dungeon full of mold and cigarette smoke with no ventilation, dirt floors covered in vomit, piss, and spit. Sam spent that night out in the van with the nanny. Then there was the abandoned warehouse in Oakland. We got there late and, though sketchy, it was comfy once we laid down our seven-foot-square raft of lashed-together sleeping bags, bed-rolls, and pillows. It wasn't until morning that we noticed the broken glass, punched-in, graffitied walls, and general filth of the place. As Andy brought the last swig of his sole beer from the night before to his lips, he remarked on his hopes that no one from family services should walk in just now.

Even in these decidedly non-child-friendly places, the people involved in getting us there or hooking us up with them were always supportive and friendly. And we all had a blast, not least of all Sam. With constant motion and stimulus as his allies, he was in his element. Surrounded by his mom, dad, and extended family 24-7, and a steady source of new faces to show off to every day, I do believe we had found a perfect milieu for the little hambone.

On the first tour, Andy and I got a stroke of good luck at the expense of some unlucky others. The band we were going to be sharing the tour with blew up their van on their way to meeting us on the West Coast. We were going to lend the other band our little car, but then decided that it made more sense for Sam, Andy, and myself to pile into the car and fill up the big cube van with the rest of the two bands, the roadie, the nanny, and other assorted hangers-on. We missed out on some impromptu dance parties and drinking sessions, but we were able to come and go as we pleased. We never had to wait for anyone with our frustrated, crying baby and could travel at our own pace.

At the shows, a revolving group of people including mom, dad, band members, and friends would hang out with Sam, either in a quiet room provided by the promoters or in the van, until we were ready to play. Our good friend and nanny, Hollie, would take Sam for the duration of our set, at which point he would promptly fall asleep in her arms. Sam would wake up and hang with whoever was around while we loaded out and drove back to our accommodations, then he'd crash again when we got there. The next day, he'd wake up at nine o'clock sharp and we'd do it all again.

In Europe we were all traveling in one van. This too had its pros and cons. Sometimes we had to wait around endlessly with a baby who was getting more frustrated and weepy by the second, but we also had many helping hands at all times. We kept the drives short, brought along a stroller, carseat, toys, snacks, books, diapers, and anything else that the discerning one-year-old could possibly desire. Sam had more luggage than the rest of the band combined.

Although the punks were outstanding everywhere, I found that Europe was more child-friendly on the whole. You could get biodegradable disposable diapers almost everywhere and they were cheap! Every gas station had a family room and a change table. We were using cloth diapers up until the tour but the idea of traveling with an ever-growing bag of shitty diapers was too much to bare. Our own collective stench was enough.

Sam started to come into his own and developed his own language. One of my best memories of the tour was of us walking down the street (seven to ten people at any given time) parroting, en masse, everything that came out of Sam's mouth. He would yell, we'd all yell, he'd yell louder, we'd all yell louder. And so on. Sam was our undisputed leader.

When I first got pregnant, amid all the confusion and excitement, I realized that I did not want the things that I enjoyed in my life to end. I wanted to keep something for myself, apart from my baby. I wanted to remain active and passionate, so I decided that I needed to keep singing, to keep on touring and stay involved in my life. Once I had Sam I became more creative and passionate about the both of us. Many things have changed about the way I do things, about the way we write music and tour, but the change is good. I feel like I'm growing and learning alongside Sam.

The only time I have to myself is when Sam is napping, down for the night, or when he's out for the day with his dad. I imagine this is a familiar litany for most mothers. The erratic schedule of finding time and energy to feed my creative impulses has led to a whole new process. Where I was once able to work on a project until it was finished or practice a song until it was complete, I now find myself working in short, sharp bursts, and the entire process is stretched out over longer and longer periods. I have had to learn great patience with myself because I often have to go running off right when the creative juices start to flow. It's not all bad though. It gives me time to reflect, plan, and look forward to the next two minutes alone with my project.

I look at single moms with one or more kids who have remained creative and vital and I stand with my hat off, my hand over my heart, and I demand a moment of silence. The strength and power of these women demands respect. It's hard enough to raise kids on your own and just get by, but to carve out a creative identity for yourself—that is truly going beyond the pale. Since having my son, I am continuously amazed by him, by myself, and by all the women who have come before me. It takes tremendous creativity, patience, and endurance to be a parent. It takes tremendous creativity, patience and endurance to remain creative, patient, and to endure.

Before Sam was born, it seemed as though I had all the time in the world. I could laze around and read all day, go out to thrift stores, or just sit and stare at the wall for hours on end. Now I am in a constant state of exhaustion, my mail has been left unanswered for over a year. Yet, I've found the time to teach myself how to use a sewing machine, I've made crazy, handmade dolls for all Sam's comrades and even made clothes for Sam. I have designed and screen-printed kid's T-shirts; I have started to paint; I have been making pieces of art out of old window frames and hand cut stencils; I have planted a flower garden for the first time. I sing, write, and tour with the band and I am a full-time stay-at-home mom. I have never been as creative in my whole life. Where there always used to be something holding me back—not having the right materials, not knowing where to start—I always had an excuse. Now there seems to be nothing holding me back. The floodgates have opened . . . unleash the chaos!

2,567 MILES

LLI WILBURN

102

HOBO POOL, saratoga Springs, Wyoming. Actually the REALLY hot spring is enclosed and it was too hot for me or Opal. This is the spring where it mixes with the creek + makes a ⁼ warm ⁼ spring. I keep on imagining people traveling here 100 years ago, cold and bashed up and weary + coming across this place. I bet at least one or two folks died happy here.

JULY 13   FREMONT LAKES, NEBRASKA

Not a good night. Noisy, crowded, buggy campground, hard ground, anthills, not a fun place to sleep. Of course that did mean I got up early enough to watch the sun rise over Lake 15. There are something like 17 lakes, all known by numbers. Opal and I swam in a lake whose number I've forgotten: thank you Bruce Springsteen + T. Coraghessan Boyle, I just call it Greasy Lake. Opal didn't mind the grease, as long as she could get into the water. I liked Lake Anita better. This place is rather nice in the morning though. On the other side of the lake are the UP tracks and a grain elevator that looks like a moated castle at night. The guy next to us says this is one of the busiest stretches of track in the country. Trains go by every 10 minutes. Now to finish my coffee, wake up Opal and leave before the RVs start rolling..

JULY 7

DROVE IN AND OUT OF OMINOUS thunder clouds All through
Pennsylvania And Ohio. Rob + Gopi mounted A camera on my
dashboard and I packed everything I'd need for the show, but
I think Opal's getting more Artwork done than me.

THE MEANS
OF PRODUCTION

J. ANDERSON COATS

THE LIBRARY is still and quiet. Dust powders thin shafts of sunlight over the frowning bust of the namesake. My son giggles and scrambles up the stairs on all fours. It is summer and all the students have gone home but I still remind him of his volume. For my next chapter I need medieval children's games and the layouts of certain towns on the Welsh marches; he carries the list of books and articles that will get me there. We climb to the third floor and get to work.

He loves the big green square on the copier and the way the light glides back and forth beneath the glass. He loves the embossed gold numbers on the journals, and counts each run in his library voice while tracing his stubby fingers over them. He asks about title pages, call numbers, and why none of my books have pictures. Together we sound out titles and he pecks them, one key at a time, into the catalog.

How much of this will he remember, I wonder, will he be twenty-one and ask about the big, silent building he'd seen at the age of three with the long aisles that begged for roller-skates and tricycles? I hope he does. It is why I bring him here.

The composition part of writing is very familiar to him, Mama at the keyboard with her fingers clacking over the ancient keys or trotting off to Saturday critique group. But writing is not stringing words together on a page. Writing is more primal than something as simple as words in patterns, aligned and arranged. Writing is the telling of a story, and it is also the production of the story. Historical fiction is a constant juxtaposition of imagination and scholarship, and the library is at the heart and soul of production.

He has come to love the college library and see it with a similar brand of wonder as the writer and historian who is his mother. The same child who must be bribed with ice cream and cartoons to give his mother an hour of uninterrupted peace to write, can spend hours in the library while she copies, scours citations, and takes volumes of notes from dusty books. The computer is his rival, a competitor for his companionship, but the act of writing is transformed in the library into something he can share in.

I might never have thought to bring him here if the amount of research required by historical fiction was not so vast and my time so limited. A three-year-old in a research library—images of scattered books, ravaged stacks, cookie crumbs, and crayon smears competed with that of the librarian escorting us out and banning me for life. Our first visit occurred through a deadline's necessity and I braced for endless whining combined with the unleashing of a bored three-year-old's destructive power. What I did not expect was the widened eyes and the awestruck gasp, the chattered litany of questions and the request to walk through every corridor of every floor. What I did not expect was for him to take to the place like the proverbial duck to water.

He's not always perfect. He often forgets his library voice, and one time got his wrist caught in the rare books cage on the second floor. He bounces on the stools to hear them squeal, and often selects random books with the conviction that I need to read them. Some days even a parade of puzzle books and plastic army men do not distract him for long, and I despair of getting any work done at all. But as I watch the dusty sun trace off his hair as he sorts my notecards by color and number, I realize that he is learning more from this place than I ever will.

When I was three, my intellectual world ended at the public library and my youthful goal was to read every book in the building. I can still remember my dismay as a teenager upon reading the last medieval book on the shelf there; my learning was at an end since I had read every book in my world. Upon seeing the rows and rows of medieval books in my first college library, the world opened up again. My own mother is an avid reader and a librarian herself, but she never had a reason to show me scholarship. She is a consumer and I am a producer, and even if my son grows up to leave production behind, he will at least know the methods for it.

At three, he devours picture books from our public library, but as he grows he will have an understanding, albeit subconscious, of the vastness of collected human knowledge. With any luck, he will also have an understanding of what it means to write. He will remember the two-hour drive and the endless swipes of the copier, the swish of highlighter and the rattle of binders. He will remember creeping out of bed to hunker at the top of the stairs, silently watching his mother's fingers flying over the keyboard far into the night, bathed in a serene electronic glow. This is his brand of love, a child's fierce and single-minded love, and perhaps that puts Mama's writing somewhere in a three-year-old's ken.

We go outside for our picnic lunch and he is a little boy again. He kicks off his shoes and chases squirrels from one stone edifice to another. Then he tries to coax them back with sandwich crusts and carrot sticks. Lingering students and the odd professor give

107

him bewildered smiles that deepen in confusion when they notice me in my ripped jeans and Birkenstocks. He is as out of place here as I am. A three-year-old in a research library is as strange to them as a teen mother in a Seven Sisters college. One who is soon to graduate magna cum laude in history with departmental honors. But this is who we are, he and I. When he is hot and tired, he gulps down blue juice from a thermos before we head inside to finish the day's research.

We take the back stairs down to the sub-basement. The library's mazelike passages and stairways enchant him and he shouts to hear the echo. He helps me wrestle an atlas the span of my arms onto the copier and we copy a map in eight sections. On the floor we spread them out and work them together like a puzzle, then tape them up. We talk about why the roads are so crooked and why the lettering is funny. I let him run his race-cars over the streets and walls of medieval London while I skim some culinary treatises and jot down recipes.

All these objects—map folios, tiny dusty chronicles with rag-paper pages, the endless runs of journals—hopefully one day he will see them as gifts. It would be easy to bring him to the zoo or the park or even let him watch Disney movies all day, but instead I bring him into my world, the world I forge with imagination and scholarship. He will not always love coming to the research library with me. In a few years he might not want to come at all, and in ten years he will ask me to drop him off a block away from the mall or the movie theater. But hopefully he will hold onto that sense of wonder in the diversity of knowledge, the curiosity of scholarship. Undoubtedly, his life will follow his own interests, but with luck, he will embrace the potential inherent in this place. With luck, he will synthesize what is expected of him with what he wants to do with his life. Much like his mother, who learned that lesson from writing.

Before he came, my life was a frenzied jumble of writing and scholarship. He joined it without missing a step and came into the world on Wednesday of spring break. I was back in class the next Monday, back with my open journal in my hospital bed. Now there is less frenzy but not much less jumble, and my trips to the library include cars, snacks, and puzzle books tossed elbow to elbow with notebooks, folders, and a bulging coin purse. He has taught me to collaborate rather than confront, to integrate rather than abandon.

Before he came, my writing desk was an ordered series of notebooks and binders, but now it is scattered with markers, stickers, and coloring books to ward away bored little fingers. There are even several articles on medieval military engineering whose page numbers are circled in meticulous blue crayon; they were left carelessly on the map table within a numerically oriented toddler's grasp. Before he came, I would have exploded at the desecration of research, but he has taught me perspective. At least he did not see the footnote numbers within the text. At least he did not find scissors or glue sticks. With that blue crayon he has proved that paper is merely paper and the facts upon it do not change with mere cosmetic alterations. The burden of historical fiction is in the telling, in the production. He has reminded me of my responsibility.

Before he came, I could only write when a certain series of events unfolded just so; if I did not eat my bagel sandwich (ham and cheddar with cheap yellow mustard) immediately after arriving home from school (after 2:50 but before 3:00), my frame of mind was simply unproductive and would remain that way for the evening. I live on shared time now, and that makes me grateful for what scraps present themselves. Writing is no longer smooth paragraphs and flowing thoughts, but fragments from this notebook and the back of that napkin, collected and compiled during that rare naptime or after he has gone to bed. He has taught me flexibility. By breaking my dependence on routine, he has freed my writing from a paralysis of meaningless ritual and infused it with a vitality that carries through to the page.

He is getting crabby. The ratty blanket appears from his little green pack and he crawls into a leather chair to suck his thumb. I feed him pretzels even though food is forbidden, and rush through my last round of copying before a racecar flies at my head. When he grows whiny, I distract him with the compact shelving and show him how the whole aisle slides back and forth with the touch of a button. He delightedly grates the naval warfare and gardening sections open and shut while I pack up ten dollars' worth of copies, a notebook full of scribbles, and a stack of books for further perusal.

The librarian greets him by name when we pile my books on the counter. She reads the titles as she scans them and asks if Conquerors and Conquered in Medieval Wales is his bedtime story.

He shakes his head. "Mama is writing her story."

"Oh really? What is her story about?"

"Castles and sword-fighting. It's in Wales."

How much of this will he remember, I wonder, as he hoists himself up to peer over the marble counter. Will he remember the endless rows of books or the compact shelving or the copier's drone? Will he remember the slick leather chairs or the catalog's series of buttons? Or will he remember little beyond the building itself, only that his mother brought him to a vast edifice full of books to push the green button on the copier and type incomprehensible words into a computer? What he has learned from the library, only he knows. But whatever that is, we have shared it. I have given him something of myself that is as important to me as he is.

Right now he loves what I love, and he sees me love to write. He sees me love to read and he sees the thread of history running through both. He sits behind my computer and writes his own stories in staple-bound chapbooks with construction-paper covers. Sometimes I let him sit on my lap and he pecks out a story from his imagination on the computer, key by tedious key. His face lights up when his words slide from the printer into his waiting hands. Whether he will keep writing remains to be seen, but he loves the act of production. Like his mother, he has learned it from writing.

He falls asleep in the car on the two-hour drive home, and not even the clamor of city traffic awakens him. In the rearview mirror he looks younger than three, a porcelain baby-doll slumped in his carseat. I think of all the times I wished him forward, wished him talking and walking and out of diapers, but now I wish he would freeze in time right now, right here, asleep in his carseat on the Schuylkill expressway. Time does not work that way, but the written word does. The written word preserves what time fades and changes, and by virtue of the written word he will always be three, eager and charming, racing up the library stairs on all fours.

That is what I will remember of this place.

109

LETTERS TO AISHA

LAURA FOKKENA

ONE OF the last times I saw your mother was in Jasmin, a basement hotel bar owned by Nasser's nephew. Every week he met with a group of exiled African princes who'd been kicked out of their respective dictatorships. Cairo was a haven for stolen wealth and European mistresses; it was here they spent every Tuesday night drinking imported scotch and mourning the good old days when it took nothing but a phone call to invade the Sudan. They used to be powerful. Now they were merely rich.

Kitty was the only woman at the table who wasn't someone's mistress. She was the Poet, which made her an honorary man. The American in me found this amusing. In my world poetry is a feminine undertaking, and the men who engage in it do it with some shame at not having played ball in high school. But here—where the tradition of the novel wasn't even adopted until the 20th century—poetry is the highest art. In Iran, before television, they used to play a game in which everyone sits in a circle and recites a line from Rumi. The letter of the last line recited by the person before you becomes the letter of the first line you recite. This game goes on for hours; every person playing it must have committed an incredible stock of poetry to memory in order to participate, but it was popular enough that it was something normal people did, you know, to spend an evening, the way we watch Seinfeld.

So Kitty was the Poet. None of the princes had read her, they only knew she was published and had won awards, and was therefore fit to sit at the table. I had read her, and could quote her, too. But I was just a girl like the European mistresses, there on the arm of a man, and mine wasn't even a king. The princes refilled my drinks and told me I was pretty. They argued world affairs and the death of communism; politically they had nothing in common with one another but their status as failed monarchs. Kitty turned away from the spoils-of-war talk to tell me I should read *The Alexandria Quartet*.

Back in America I took her typewritten manuscripts and vowed to get them published in the U.S., but I lost them all when my hard drive crashed. My back-ups were on disks as ancient and corrupted as the nose of the Sphinx. I blamed Napoleon. Not because he was responsible, but because it just seemed fitting.

*   *   *

It's been six months to the day since I learned of her death. You've been living with this for over a year now, a situation I find almost impossible to process, and I end up feeling guilty for having a full year of thinking she was alive when in fact she wasn't—a luxury you, of course, could not share. Delayed mourning.

But you're only six years old. I hear children recover quickly from such trauma, though I have my doubts.

I spent that year making exasperated phone calls to three states searching for news. I knew you'd moved, but had no address. Still, your mom had mine and had promised to contact me first. I couldn't understand what was taking her so long. I spent one surreal night talking to a stranger in Oregon whose only connection was the fact that she shared the surname of one of your mother's many pseudonyms. She listened to me, three time-zones distant, politely straining for a common link and me reaching, ridiculously, for points of contact: Her name was Kitty, she was a poet, she lived with her mother, had a daughter named Aisha. I knew it was futile but I didn't want to hang up. I didn't want to stop talking about her, and for a good twenty minutes this stranger was willing to listen. I'll be forever thankful for that, however pointless the conversation was in retrospect. By that time you'd already moved back to California with your grandmother, and your mother, my friend, whose wisdom saved me countless times, was already gone.

*   *   *

Kitty and I used to meet at Il Capo, an Italian restaurant in Zamalek, the island in the Nile where my daughter was conceived. It was run by Nisha, a distant relative of some former prince or pasha whose palace had been confiscated by the government and turned into the Marriott. Nisha was in Cairo waiting to collect a settlement. And just when you think that story can't get any more imperialist, he had a girlfriend from Texas. (I couldn't invent these tales if I tried. As Isabel Allende says, the trouble with fiction is that it must seem credible, when reality rarely is.)

I wrote straight journalism back then, interviews with local musicians, historical features about forgotten pockets of the city. Your mom wrote poetry. The magazine I wrote for got wind of her work and wanted to print it, but she was skeptical. Kitty had never seen the point of publishing. It was the artistry she was after, not the business side of things; the thought of conference calls and marking time by fiscal years put her off. She called herself a poet because she wrote poetry, and when other people came to her house she'd read it to them and tell them that next time they came over they should bring their own. They always did. Especially the seventeen-year-old girls who still lived at home, who were studying engineering at their parents' insistence, or the British accountant who was in the Middle East to save money and had never thought of doing something creative.

She confessed to me that she had friends back in southern California who called themselves poets because they'd published something several years ago, but they otherwise lived utterly conventional lives in their pant suits and three-car garages. She didn't understand how people in such circumstances could think of themselves as poets when their lives had no poetry in them at all. She and a girlfriend once filled a psychiatrist full of opium just to get him to stop listening and start talking. Even Christina, my roommate, who distrusted all my friends and their decadent ways, asked "Who is that woman?" after meeting Kitty and for an hour being the focus of someone's intense interest, someone who didn't know or care whether or not she ever went to graduate school. "Can we see her again?" she asked.

Hypnotic.

Your mother's aversion to publishing notwithstanding, other friends put her in contact with the magazine. Even then she called me half an hour before her meeting with the editor, wondering if it was really all that important that she followed through on this stuff—plus, she couldn't find anything to wear. I told her to go anyway and, to my surprise, she did. There were six editors and photographers waiting for her and after the issue came out strangers recognized her on the street. I only know this because she'd tell me about "this fascinating woman I met outside the Khan . . ." with the whole getting-recognized story a prelude to the real saga, which was that this fascinating woman lives on a houseboat outside Kitkat Square and doesn't know what to do about her unintended pregnancy, so we're meeting tomorrow at the coffeeshop to talk about it, she's an artist, you know, and Kitty, how do you get these stories out of total strangers?

Thing is, though, I fell into it, too, and there wasn't anything mysterious about it. No one turns their back on someone giving them permission to be passionate.

* * *

"Is her real name Kitty?" my daughter asked me, in bed, the night after I found out she had died. It was all I could talk or think about for twenty-four hours, and in a way it became Rakaya's first conscious experience with death, although she'd never met Kitty.

"No"—I always vowed I'd never tell her this because I didn't want her getting ideas, but—"when she was nine she told her parents she was going to burn the house down if they didn't let her change it."

"Wow," Rakaya said, impressed. I knew it was coming, you could see the wheels turning in her head, and I think I told her just because I needed the predictability of hearing her say it: "Could I do that? Tell you I'll burn down the house if you don't let me do something?"

"No," I said, because I'm her mother and that's the kind of things mothers tell their children, you know, study hard, mind your manners, don't burn the house down when you don't get your way. What I didn't tell her was that I'd had the same thought when Kitty told me that story originally. Can people do that? Could I have done that?

*   *   *

Her second husband was Egyptian and reluctantly took her to Cairo.

"You'll hate it," he warned. "You'll loath it. The streets, the grime, everyone in your business."

But she pushed and she pushed and eventually he acquiesced. They left Paris and moved to Egypt, where she proved him right. She hated it, loathed it, the streets, the grime, everyone in her business. But she was never one to responsibly veer into the familiar, and spent the next dozen years in the Middle East. Her life in Cairo outlasted her marriage, though they didn't divorce right away lest she lose her residency. Egypt's polygamy laws allowed him to take another wife and everyone was happy, or at least content, with the arrangement.

She enrolled in the American University's MA program in Arab Art and Architecture and was writing a thesis on the doors of mosques in Syria, an endeavor that was eroding her sanity piece by piece, brick by brick. She was raised Jewish, she told me, but had converted to Islam and joined a Sufi order which she ended up hating because it was too conservative. But what can you do? Go back to America? She lived over a mosque and had a love-hate relationship with the muezzin.

All this was done on the back of a semi-aristocratic background, the kind my Protestant Midwestern self didn't know existed anymore. I can only romanticize it up to a certain point because I realize that sliding around the globe in gold bangles and ballet slippers on a quest to find some 14th-century Sufi text that's rumored to be available only in Damascus, and then only if you know someone, isn't the kind of thing everyone would want to do even if they could afford it, and most of them, including me, can't. She read Edward Said and said she was an Orientalist anyway, a philosophy that was tolerated by even my most political friends because they appreciated her honesty and her engagement and probably also because she'd had love affairs with some of them.

Can you do that? She was enchanted with the notion of salons, enchanted with the impressionists and all the writers under voluntary exile in Paris in the 1920s. Unfortunately she was living in the wrong era, since most of us thought of everything we did in terms of how it would play on a resume. Even my nights in her apartment get a line now; 1991-1992: Year Abroad, American University in Cairo. 1993: Cairo, conducted independent research on gender politics in the Middle East. For the rest of us everything had to be marked and defined and we naturally approached others that way, too: "What do you do? What are you studying?" By that we didn't mean we cared, we meant where are you on the totem pole? How are you properly contextualized? But for Kitty it was all about finding someone's inner core, and you can't do that if you're fooling around asking them if they've declared a major yet.

*   *   *

I call your grandmother a few weeks after I get the news. She speaks with your mother's cadence and it makes me want to keep talking to her about anything at all, even though it's past midnight and the candle's out and both our babies are asleep, you at the edge of the Pacific Ocean and my own daughter here on the Atlantic.

"It was a year ago now," she says. January 2002. This relieves me because I know I spoke to Kitty in October or so. To know that there might have been a long stretch of time in which I could have found her if I'd just tried harder—that was destroying me more than anything.

You know what's ridiculous? One of my first thoughts, in that split second when everything piles up and messages criss-cross and overlap without reason, was, "She died?!—I can't believe she didn't call me! "

It's almost too bizarre to report, but it's true; it was my first reaction. To think she'd staged something as grand as her own death without telling me? I thought we were friends!

*   *   *

But I'm leaving things out. The phone calls, mainly, which always started with "Laura, I'm in a big depression. . . ." My husband and I became armchair psychologists, diagnosing a hundred maladies and another hundred cures. First we told her to take her studies more seriously, then we reversed ourselves and told her to abandon them completely. We told her that her friends and relationships were too demanding, or that perhaps she should get a job to have something to do. The university was hiring English teachers for Eritrean refugees, and your mother was more than qualified. Maybe she needed more iron. In one desperate moment I suggested buying a radio. "How can you live without music?"

But with each diagnosis she would only shake her head and say, "It's Cairo, it's Cairo. It eats you up." At which point we of course said she should move to Greece, or go back to Paris, even home to Los Angeles. She was adamantly opposed to this last suggestion, and told me of a time back in California when she and her first husband were living in a boxy apartment complex and another woman's husband came into her flat at the end of the working day. "Hi, honey, I'm home!" he called, just like her own husband did every day at the same time, and he began to fix himself a sandwich before he realized he was in the wrong house, so identical were their lives to those of their neighbors.

"That's when I decided I couldn't stay there," she said, though her view would eventually change because of you.

Her son and her first husband managed better with this. They were mathematically inclined, she said, capable of working out complex theories without thought to the aesthetics of their surroundings. Her son was about my age. He had just finished high school and found a good job working with computers. She altered between pride in his accomplishments and her wish that he would worry less about algorithms and more about seeing the world. She wanted him to go to college and study something obscure and impractical, or take a year off to live in Prague. "He's so young!" she'd cry. "He should use this time to explore." She worried that a whole life lived in an office would turn him into one of those retirees who purchases kitchen gadgetry and recreational vehicles and takes a personal stake in the fates of game show contestants.

Your brother also made an appearance in every conversation involving regret. "I never raised my son," she'd say, her voice trailing off. It was the one part of her past that I struggled with. Objectively, intellectually, and politically I know that fathers are as capable as mothers when it comes to parenting, but on some other plane I'm unable to imagine giving up my child, her best interests notwithstanding. How did she do it? And why?

After the divorce, she said, she kept him with her for several months, but her living situation was chaotic, she had no money and her depression was at its height. "One afternoon I found myself sitting on this hardback chair, the baby at my breast, and I just started sobbing, because I knew I couldn't do it." Her ex had a house and a stable job.

It's the first time I think of parental sacrifice in these terms. Motherhood, in all its messy gut-wrenching reality, isn't only what we create, but what we're capable of relinquishing. I find this hard to face.

On my twenty-first birthday I admitted how much I wanted a baby. Most people who heard this confession—which is how I thought of it at the time—could barely contain their disdain at someone so young threatening to reproduce, but your mother nodded in understanding. "You feel you have a lot to give," she said. "I think you should do it."
A few weeks later I left for America on what was supposed to be a two-month trip to take a class and sort out my financial aid. To everyone's surprise, most especially my own, I found out I was pregnant and forfeited my return ticket. My husband arrived at the beginning of my second trimester, and, although we continued with our marathon telephone conversations for several years, neither one of us saw your mom again.

One night she called me from California. She'd abandoned her MA program, stole your father from his pyramids and minarets, and was back in L.A., surrounded by palm trees and strip malls and pregnant with you. She was in her mid-forties by then, once again reinventing herself with a new name, a new husband, a new landscape. "Crazy, isn't it?" she asked.

"You have a lot to give," I answered.

*   *   *

Your name comes from Aisha Bint Abu-Bakr, Muhammad's favorite wife. "Get half of your religion from this red one," he is said to have admonished his followers.

Do you have red hair, like your mother? I asked her once as we compared the features of our children, certain that Kitty's genes would burn through the dominant impulses of your North African father.

But no. "Aisha's hair is dark and her skin is olive." Like Rakaya's. We give our daughters the last names of their fathers as is required by Egyptian law, see our faces disappear, and wonder if our influence will disappear with them, our presence forever recessive.

*   *   *

Back in America, I would call her in a panic. "I can't get anything done," by which I of course meant anything cool. Even the straight journalism I'd written in Cairo felt like an artistic outlet, but now having a baby meant writing for pay or not at all. Fifty dollars for a column about the Algerian elections, another forty for a piece about the new library downtown. If I could write the whole story in an hour it was actually good money, but spend too much time thinking and delivering the newspapers paid more than writing for them. Lounging about putting words on paper became a shameful indulgence, like buying disposable diapers instead of the cloth kind, or using the television as a babysitter.

Certainly I could make this work if I could only find that elusive thing called "balance." I'd get up at 5:30, I promised myself each night, as all those old male authors who write books on writing suggested. I'd read the optional reading for all my classes, write a novel, make oil paintings, I'd take up yoga! It was a schedule that seemed disciplined in theory, but the fact was I was already up at dawn every day, which made the whole endeavor pointless. Apparently those old male authors who prided themselves on their work ethic weren't shoved awake each morning by half-starved toddlers scrambling up their nightshirts looking for a bite to eat.

"Stop thinking in moderation," Kitty told me, "and start thinking in waves." She said every creative endeavor has periods of input and output. "It's like inhaling and exhaling. You spend time learning and thinking and working stuff out in your brain." Weeks, months, years. "In those times it looks like nothing's happening, but that's when all the major questions are being answered," she said. "And then you exhale, and put all that effort into something tangible." Like a book, or a class, or something you build or invent. "And" (the inevitable) "I think you're just in an inhale period right now."

*   *   *

It's hard to imagine someone so delicate changing diapers. Your mother moved like the poetry she wrote, graceful, precise. But she did have strong ideas about parenthood. She rebelled against vaccinations, for example, and was a fierce opponent of circumcision, her Jewish upbringing notwithstanding. "A boy's first experience of the world should not be intense pain in his penis," she said, one of the better arguments against the practice I've ever heard.

"They'll forget it the next morning," the doctors told her, and I laugh at this, the idea of someone trying to convince Kitty that we forget pain.

Is this where her chronic cough came from? "Excuse me, Laura," she'd sputter, and I'd hear the phone land with a clunk on the kitchen counter. Breathe, I prayed, hearing her gasp in the background. She'd return with a glass of water and tell me it's okay, but you could hear the fragility of her constitution in her throat, her soprano voice breaking into spasms without warning.

"When things were really bad I considered suicide," she confessed one quiet night in Cairo, "but I could never leave my mother." Ten years later pneumonia makes the decision for her, and her mother is left alone regardless.

But, of course, that's not true, either. Your grandmother still has your brother, and you. And she has all your mother's writing.

*   *   *

I saved the mangled hard drive full of her poetry for sentimental reasons, the way I saved the red scarf that smelled of her perfume. Years later, one particularly dedicated friend spent his Thanksgiving vacation restoring it. Nevertheless, it took several months for me to hit upon the right combination of keywords that, when inserted into the search engine, would bypass hundreds of other corrupted files and bring her words back to me. The right combination happened to be "second day of the war." As bombs fell over Baghdad in March of 2003, I remembered the poem she'd written about the first Gulf War in 1991: Gilgamesh come to greet them, Holy warrior, repulse us now.

My friend's computer expertise—the kind she had once lamented in her son—was ultimately what brought her artistry back to me, a melding of two worlds I know she would appreciate. By then it had been almost two months since I'd learned of her death. Her words scrolled by me like an ancient oracle, the search engine ticking away mechanically. I could barely breathe. Odes to Paris and Baghdad and Damascus, and many more to Cairo—for an infinity I surrendered to you, city of Pharaohs—and, most of all, to your father, her young Egyptian lover who would eventually follow her back to America against his better judgment: I watched your shadow and saw it wince.

Though her body is gone she's left you a record of her life, a record of your father's guarded heritage seen through the release of her Californian eyes, and, perhaps, a store of maternal advice, so that in times of doubt you can consult your mother and she will speak to you in her own words, both as an artist and a woman:

> A solitary boat cuts through a glistening black Nile, and I remembered the soul lodged tenuously between the cavity of the chest and the membranes of the head, and the voices of caution to conceal what is precious. However, I choose to throw all my cards to those feverish winds, for to withhold, one ceases to live, one begins to die. And awe this life, this crazy dance, it moves so very quickly.

DON'T FORGET THE LUNCHES . . .

MONICA BOCK & ZOFIA BURR

WELL BEFORE I had actually given birth, my first major body of artwork—as a graduate student at he School of the Art Institute of Chicago—was about birth. Thinking about family in the context of the debate over abortion, I produced a series of mixed-media objects that became an installation for my 1990 MFA exhibition. The centerpiece of the installation, a round oak table set with four miniature place settings, was called *The Uterus and its Appurtenances from Behind*. With language and anatomical imagery lifted from my mother's anatomy texts, the piece was built on memories of her struggle between work and family. Doll plates laid with miniature cast sterling internal organs suggested the personal toll behind decorous housekeeping, as well as the reality of life consumed in life. The piece came out of knowing that, like my mother, my need for my own work was coupled with a desire to birth and raise children, that I would soon be negotiating the same treacherous territory between intimacy and autonomy that she had, and that I would be equally torn and driven.

Three years later, I gave birth to my daughter at home, and shortly thereafter, made a small piece called *Shadow Wrestling*, using two bars of glycerin soap resting on end face-to-face on a reliquary stand encasing a small vile of my own blood. Originally based on a Theresa of Avila quote about "wrestling with the shadow of death," the piece marked my first use of glycerin as a reference to flesh and its vulnerability, and offered itself as a contemplation of the impermanence that's felt specifically when looking at

one's children. In part, my understanding of the piece was shaped well after it was made by a poem written for it by my friend Zofia Burr, a writer and professor of English at George Mason University. We met in 1995, when we were both living in Chicago. I was pregnant with my second child, and Zofia and I got to talking about home birth. At that time, Zofia was recently married and becoming increasingly aware of the complexity of her long-standing decision not to have children.

So we started a conversation that gradually turned into an artistic collaboration— about family, work, gender, the body, productivity, nurturing. It's essentially a conversation about taking possession of the terms of our existence, as women, as daughters, as artists, as married bisexuals, as mothers and as not-mothers, and we are both mothers and not-mothers in relation to the needs of other people in our lives. Lately our collaboration has focused on how the roles of mother and of not-mother are part of the same impossible set of expectations confronting women who choose to be defined both by work and nurturing. In regard to "the maternal body," no woman gets to define herself completely outside the terms of good mother/ bad mother—the terms of what it means to take on, tamper with, or reject the role of the mother as cultural institution.

In hindsight, it's become significant that our conversation began with home birth. It turns out, of course, that choosing home birth was just the beginning of figuring out what kind of mother I would be in relation to my work and the dominant culture's image of family. A lot of that figuring has been done in conversation with Zofia, including the decision, almost immediately after my son was born, to pursue my current tenure-track job as professor of art at the University of Connecticut, just when I thought I wanted to relax and enjoy my newborn. As Zofia says, I blame her for my getting the job I always wanted.

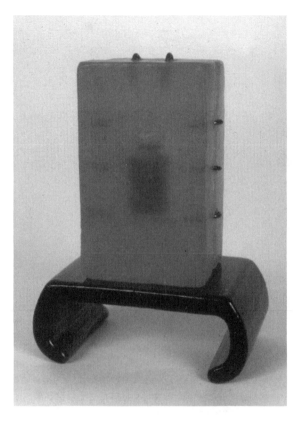

Since more or less simultaneously becoming a mother and full-time professor of art, my most recent creative work has developed as a way of talking about motherhood and childhood in a climate that all but denies their relevance. Early in my tenure process, and with the example of other mothering artists in academia, I began to realize that the complexities of family life would not easily be recognized as pertinent to my ambitions for my work. But what I am largely consumed and fascinated by are the challenges my two small children present to my adult reality and to the institutional cultures that make no place for them.

So, it became imperative to make art with and about my children, in order to make our reality known, but also to stay close to them even though half the time it's the work that preempts my actually being with them. It's an indirect kind of nurturing that can feel a lot like preoccupied neglect, as I struggle with my need for discipline when I'd rather go play, and my guilt when I'd rather not go play. Total absorption in the process of raising children (which would make me a good mother) is something I have never been able to choose. I keep choosing this kind of complex and conflicted nurturing with reflection upon nurturing, this kind of looking and public revelation of my looking, even at what may be considered un-motherly to look at (which makes me a bad mother.)

In the summer of 1998, I created a mixed-media piece called *Afterbirth (Sac Fluid Cord),* in which three cast glycerin dustpans rest on a shelf with a glass bottle encased in each of their handles. The first bottle carries a bit of amniotic sac, the next amniotic

fluid, and the last umbilical cord—my own children's birth matter. The creation of *Afterbirth (Sac Fluid Cord)* triggered the conception of a number of objects and installations linked by the title *Afterbirth(s)* and by the concept of exposing aspects of family life, or life after birth, as it were.

Maternal Exposure (don't forget the lunches), the major installation in this new body of work, has become the centerpiece of a number of solo shows including an exhibition at Mobius in Boston. The piece is inspired by the daily ritual—that I became intensely aware of when my children entered all day toddler care and pre-school—of exposing one's children and one's nurturing skills to public scrutiny. The piece consists of 418 lead sheet bags, embossed with the daily menus of school and day camp lunches I prepared for my two young children over the course of the year from January 6 to December 23, 1999. The lead bags gather in rows in one half of the exhibition space, spreading across the floor in the order the original lunches were prepared. Inserted intermittently, small lead sheet plaques replace lunch bags and announce the days when no lunches needed to be made—sick days, snow days, holidays, parties at school. As flesh-like counter-parts to the protective yet poisonous lead bags, 428 cast glycerin soap bags (equaling the number of days my children left the house for school, lunch bag in hand or not) accumulate organically on the floor in the other half of the space.

Maternal Exposure (don't forget the lunches) also represents the second collaboration in which Zofia and I have explored the conjunction of text, object, and space. It was for a 1998 installation called *Humours* that I first consciously set in motion a feedback loop in which I make or propose to make something and Zofia writes in response. For *Humours*, Zofia's poem was stamped letter by letter into the lead-sheathed architecture of the piece. For *Maternal Exposure*, Zofia wrote in response to phone conversations and a studio-visit with me while I was making the piece. As her own mother became seriously ill soon after we began, it was a particularly fraught moment that yielded poems exploring some of the more treacherous and costly meanings of maternal nurturing. For exhibition, Zofia pencils the series of poems (or poem fragments) in her own hand on the walls of the gallery surrounding the lunch bags on the floor, and "speaks" the text by way of a CD recording that plays intermittently into the space:

DEDICATION

This is for the bad mother in me I love
wanting to be kept. For
the Bad mother I love—wanting

(My mother said)
If you plan to run away, let me know and I'll pack you a lunch,
if you want to run away, let me know and I'll pack your bag.
Just be sure
to send us a postcard.

Just be sure to let me know.

The lunch bag is loaded. With coming from home that is her
carried into the world. That you are returning to. Regarded.
And what is spoken in the lunch packed and eaten,
rejected or thrown away, every day a mother is supposed
to allow the time to keep nothing of.

Nothing of what you are
returning
to loved.
Nothing of what you are returning.

A mother is supposed to allow the time to keep nothing of her
Gift. no return returned. Mother made—made mother—
no more days off from the world.
Designed against time.
To be saved Someone is of you on you
with you you are for.
Warned.

A mother is supposed to allow the time
a mother is supposed to allow the time to keep
a mother is supposed to allow the time to keep nothing
a mother is supposed to allow the time to keep nothing of her
a mother is supposed to allow the time to keep nothing of her gift

She was nurturing, and violent. She wanted.

The lunch bag is loaded. With coming from her.

During Summer '00, the lunch bags were exhibited as *Don't forget the lunches* at Real Art Ways in Hartford, CT. In this version, the lunch bags are accompanied by a new video piece called *Sibling Dance (I won't let you go)*. Silently projected large and askew in the corner behind the mass of lunch bags, the piece is a five-minute repeating narrative of two children together, dancing on the verge of conflict, and separately in the throws of tantrums. When the video is exhibited in isolation, the panting breath of a woman in labor and the cries of children in fury structure the rapid pace of the inter-cut images. At the end, the voice of the mother ("I won't let you go") and the cries of the newborn repeat in the dark. The video was created with the collaborative assistance of Steven Harper, video artist, and colleague at the University of Connecticut, who offered these thoughts when the video was completed:

When I watched the tapes that [Monica] had been making of Tristan and Thea in their home, I was uncomfortable. I was shocked to see children shove and jerk each other to the point of tears and then, minutes later, embrace and continue to dance as though no harm or shame had been done. I was surprised at her willingness to record and display these events, in such an unattended, unadorned, and therefore, seemingly, unapologetic manner . . . The discomfort I felt as I continued to watch met a notion that I shouldn't be watching. Each response hinted to the taboos surrounding the disclosure of these charged but mundane, significant but transient, familial interactions.

Another recent installation in this body of maternal work, *Afterbirths: King and Queen (Because Your Mother Said So)* is based on two charcoal drawings, one of a king and the other a queen, that my daughter furtively made on a pillar in the student exhibition pit in my department. For the installation, I traced the images in charcoal from slides of the original drawings projected large on a wall. As the original drawings were no more than three inches high, these images monumentalize evidence of a child's mark in the adult world. In front of the images is built a castle of glycerin-cast children's blocks. In each of a number of the castle's foundation blocks is embedded a lead-cast letter, with the blocks arranged to spell out the phrase "Because Your Mother Said So."

In the Fall of '99 I created a Faculty Show of *Afterbirth* pieces at the University of Connecticut's Benton Museum. *Afterbirths: Domestic Provocation*, was performed again as part of a Spring '00 solo exhibition at ArtWorks! in New Bedford, MA. The piece is an on going project based on my children's habit of "defacing" walls in our home. In the first manifestation of this project at the Benton, my children drew on the gallery walls with cast-lead sticks kept on a small salt cast shelf. Their work trespassed into the space below my "legitimate" artwork on the walls, with unexpected sensitivity to the scale and articulation of the architecture. Like *King and Queen*, the project deals with children's challenge to adult authority, but also with their creative expression as "art" in it's own right, questioning the distinction between child's play and adult work.

In the Benton Installation, *Domestic Provocation* was enacted underneath two works of mine, hanging diagonally across the gallery from each other. In *Afterbirth: Three Years Postpartum*, a cast salt frame with sheet-lead matting holds a 16x20 print of an image under glass. In *Afterbirth: Postpartum Miniature,* a tiny print of the same image displayed in a gold-plated silver frame rests on a doily on a small shelf. The image is of my son's placenta, kept frozen since his birth in 1995. Both "portraits" reflects my effort to preserve the experience of labor and the memory of new birth, but they also call attention to this phenomenal organ.

Interestingly, more than the actual birth material included in for example *Afterbirth (Sac Fluid Cord)*, this photograph of placenta and the word "afterbirth" itself have elicited discomfort, disgust, and even outrage from some viewers. One father of an art student, who visited the Fall '99 Faculty Exhibition, was appalled after reading the title of the work and realizing the image wasn't just a picture of a piece of meat. Without seeing this image at all, the board of directors at ArtWorks! objected to the artistic director's proposed show of the maternal work, until she promised to separate the words "after" and "birth" in my titles, to avoid the literal reference and emphasize the metaphor. I preferred to drop the "afterbirth" prefix rather than have the titles manipulated.

Postpartum Miniature showed at ArtWorks!, but the director couldn't risk *Three Years Postpartum* in her particular community. Aesthetically composed as this photograph is, I understand the image pushes sanitized notions of birth. For me, it represents my son, but it also represents my ownership of the pregnancy and birth process. I own this placenta because of my children's home births. Perhaps because of the apparent persistence and ease of disseminating textual and photographic evocations of the body, or because of the sheer power of naming, the word and the image in combination are taken as more dangerous than the vulnerable material itself. I keep wondering how much of this is squeamishness, and how much is fear of the empowerment the image represents.

I was recently invited to speak in a colleague's class on women in the arts, and took the opportunity to show most of the work I've discussed here. While many reactions from students were quite positive, later a few of students in the class's online message board expressed a great deal of discomfort with the work, questioning not only the images I chose but my mothering as well. In a recent *New York Times* review of the lunch bag installation, an older male critic praised the work as a remarkable testament to a mother's devotion, but criticized the politicizing wall label in which the lead was described as a metaphor for maternal ambivalence. I've heard, too, that the question of conflict between a woman's work and her family is no longer an issue, that women no longer need to choose one or the other—so why investigate further?

What I know, and what the mothers who respond so positively to these installations know, is that the conflict is inseparable from the choice. Every minute of everyday a mother makes an emotionally fraught choice between autonomy and intimacy, and every adult who reacts to this work carries stories of their own about those choices. What disturbs me is the fact that I look at my children with enough detachment to make art about us; what disquiets is the critical reflection on mothering by the mother herself. And it's a risk of a certain kind to bring ambivalence forward as the condition of ones work.

ON MOTHERING AND WRITING

RACHEL HALL

It was as Mother that woman was fearsome; it is in maternity that she must be transfigured and enslaved.

—Simone de Beauvoir

Because young humans remain dependent upon nurture for a much longer period than other mammals, and because of the division of labor long established in human groups, where women not only bear and suckle but are assigned almost total responsibility for children, most of us know both love and disappointment, power and tenderness, in the person of a woman.

—Adrienne Rich

I AM pregnant at the same time as Madonna and Helen Hunt's character, Jamie, on *Mad About You*. This season, it seems that pregnancy, motherhood, and infants are cool. And noteworthy, too: Several weeks after my daughter is born, the White House holds a press conference on speech development in infants. A panel of experts says that parents should sing and talk to even the youngest of infants because verbal stimulation is crucial to thinking and language skills. A photograph in the local paper captures Bill Clinton, his eyes cast down, his hands clasped together as if in prayer. Mothers are instructed to talk and sing to their infants because "it lays a foundation for the child's life, and in turn, our nation's future." As I read the articles, I'm uneasy. Of course I will chatter at my daughter, sing her ridiculous rhymes, learn to speak my thoughts out loud, though I am a person accustomed to quiet and introspection. But the limelight is perplexing, the attention misleading. At the time, I can't put my finger on why, exactly, but it feels like additional pressure, a new theory to add to all the other theories of how a mother ought to behave. While I am absorbing all these theories, dealing with sleep deprivation and the monotony of life with an infant, a silence descends on me, though I don't yet recognize it as such. All I know is that I am too tired to write more than a few sentences in my journal, and only sporadically. Even the journal entries look self-conscious to me now, as if I were thinking of audience—who would read these entries? Whose life was I charting here, my own or my daughter's? And there is a tension, too, in the entries, between my desire to keep track of things (nursing times, number of wet diapers, hours slept) and my desire to make sense of things.

When my daughter is six weeks old, I need to go to my office at the college where I teach to turn in some independent study grades. I have to time the forty-minute commute around nursing. This is the first time I will enter my office, the department, as a mother. I'm self-conscious, unsure of the rules, both wanting and fearing the attention and fuss. The drive goes well, and it instills confidence. I'm entering the department when I run into a former student, a fiction writer who I appreciate for his honest, subtle language and intuitive sense of plot.

"Hey, Chris," I say.

"Hi, how are you?" he asks, slowing to look into my baby carrier.

"Good," I say, "but exhausted."

"So this is your little bundle of joy," he says.

I check his face, expecting his ironic grin. Bundle of joy?

I can't allow my daughter, who is, at two months, already a personality, with particular gestures and squeals, to be turned into a cliché, anymore than I can stomach the implication that the experience of motherhood is wholly joyful. "This is the hardest thing I've ever done," I tell Chris, perhaps a bit too fiercely, for he begins to back away.

It would be untruthful to the profession of motherhood, already so underrated, to say that it's a breeze. And yet, if I don't say it's all great, then I'm perceived as unnatural, unmaternal, perverse. I know, vaguely, that I'm up against more than Chris here, but I push on. I tell Chris how consuming motherhood is, how filled with worry and fear and the unknown, how chaotic. I notice he's nodding politely, his eyes glazed over, probably thinking of his next class, or how he'd like to smoke a cigarette.

Months later, a friend mentions that television sitcoms suffer a drop in ratings after an infant is introduced into the story line, a fact she's acquired from an Entertainment Weekly she perused in the pediatrician's office. I think, *that's part of what was happening that day: mothers and babies are uninteresting beyond some temporary slapstick or cliché.* I'd been offered a script that day too and I rejected it, though it would be a long time before I knew how to say what needed to be said.

In *Of Woman Born*, Adrienne Rich writes that "Women have been both mothers and daughters but have written little on the subject; the vast majority of literary and visual images of motherhood come to us filtered through the collective or individual male consciousness. As soon as a woman knows that a child is growing in her body, she falls under the power of theories, ideals, archetypes, descriptions of her new existence, almost none of which have come from other women (though other women may transmit them) and all of which have floated invisibly about her since she first perceived herself to be female and therefore potentially a mother." The result is what she calls *The Great Silence*. Twenty years later, Jane Smiley, a mother of three, makes a similar comment in her essay "Can Mothers Think?" Writing about literature, she asks, "Where were the mothers? Why didn't they speak up? Can mothers actually think and speak?" The absence of mothers' voices in our literature, Smiley and Rich assert, is detrimental for both for the individual mother and for the culture. I'm beginning to see that my silence might be temporary, bolstered as I am by the writing of other women who found ways to face their silence—I'm writing this now, for instance. But I suspect that the silence is tenacious, rearing up again, as thick and tightly woven and startling as the first time. And I wonder what might be done to prevent it from descending at all.

129

Becoming a mother involves what psychologists call "role adjustment," and it is easy to imagine the visuals for this process: the young woman tossing aside her dark suits, her attaché case, and heels in favor of jeans, a stain-hiding turtleneck, Keds, and a quilted diaper bag. Drumroll, please: Ladies and gentleman, a new mother! In my case, I gave up vintage dresses of delicate fabric—old rayons and silks—dangling earrings, velvet scarves, and sheer beaded blouses and donned the standard issue stretch pants and loose T-shirts, things quickly pulled on and off, lifted for nursing, and easily laundered. How strange it felt after years of artful dressing to encounter the world in this utilitarian costume.

The psychological shift is more nuanced and gradual than the physical shift I've just described, but just as dramatic. What I once knew, I'm no longer sure of; what I once liked, I no longer care for, things I yearned for and hoped to achieve seem like someone else's dreams—remote, slightly foolish, pie-eyed. Recently, I gave my students in a writing workshop a journal-writing exercise. "Write me a letter," I said, "telling me what you believe in." This was a tough assignment, I thought, so I was surprised to see them writing without hesitation, their heads bent over their notebooks. I tried to write such a letter myself, but the only thing I found I believed in was that pediatricians over-prescribe antibiotics for ear infections.

When I sat down to write before becoming a mother, I was accustomed to a certain degree of self-doubt and insecurity, but I didn't doubt my material. After my daughter was born, the material which I was most interested in exploring in writing—the physical, psychological, and emotional demands of caring for a child—had been trivialized and romanticized to the point of myth. And that myth, I was learning, wasn't to be messed with. If one can't write about her passion, what is there to write about? Put differently: why write?

It is a dreary February afternoon in western New York. Melting snow and mud pool by my students' booted feet. The plastic stapled to the classroom windows to keep the cold air out snaps and billows in the wind. In this beginning creative-writing class, the students, in two groups of twelve, are turning in their first fiction-writing assignment. We have to distribute them to each other quickly in order to get to the discussion of two published stories. As I do every semester, I have given the class explicit directions about coming prepared with the right number of copies, already stapled and labeled. But in one group, only two people are prepared. The rest are madly collating on their desks tops. At eight months pregnant, I can no longer wedge myself into these desks, and have had to ask a student to bring me the armchair from behind the lectern. Papers slip off the students' desk tops, sail through the air, and land on the scuffed wood floor. Someone asks if I have a stapler on me.

I'm tired from carrying around an extra twenty-five pounds, from waking every couple hours at night to pee. "No, I don't have a stapler," I say measuredly. "I thought I asked you guys to come prepared."

I catch the eyes of one student, a young man whose writing and comments show promise. I intend to encourage him to take more writing classes. But his eyes startle me; they are steely, contemptuous. I imagine he is thinking "Pregnant bitch," "Cow," "What's the big deal?" Behind me, the heater grinds loudly and clicks on. When I look back, the student is bent over his papers again. I don't know what to say. I am no longer who I think I am. My new girth, the loose smock and stretch pants are speaking for me, telling people who I am, what I am, and in this role I am supposed to be patient and undemanding, uncritical and unconditionally loving. I'm aware of something else, too, another transgression: I have brought my body—my clumsy, swollen, female body—into the classroom, called attention to the fact that I am a woman in a place where man is still the norm.

Fortunately or unfortunately, there are plenty of "experts" who will happily tell me who I am, what I should expect once I am expecting. I study these magazines and books, just as I mooned over *Teen, Young Miss, Seventeen*, and *Mademoiselle* in junior high, absorbing the guidelines, the fashion dos and don'ts, the credo of young womanhood. Both the magazines for teens and mothers have articles and regular columns on relationships, diet, and make-up tips. Both are laden with advertisements and checklists of things the reader needs: things for the nursery, things to take to the hospital. The layette, that lovely French word co-opted by American materialism, comes to mean a confusing assortment of little cotton items—some with snaps, some with booties, some with hoods and drawstrings. I buy them all, checking off the list efficiently as I go. And just as the magazines recommend, our freezer is packed with soups and sauces for easy meals after the baby is born. It doesn't strike me then, as it does now, how I was groomed for motherhood by those teen magazines. Nor do I note the revealing fact that the word "teenager" became popular in the fifties, as did this particular, and tenacious, incarnation of motherhood. I can't think this because I am too busy preparing and later too busy deciphering my daughter's cries. Is she gassy? Hungry? Tired? Wet? Generally alarmed with the sharp edges, the hard realities of the world after nine months suspended in a watery pouch?

I'm looking around for a story to add to a class packet, when I come across Alice Munro's "Labor Day Dinner." The protagonist, a children's book illustrator and mother of two girls, wonders why she hasn't been able to get to her work. "Roberta meant to keep busy illustrating books. Why hasn't she done this? No time, nowhere to work: no room, no light, no table. *No clear moments of authority, now that life has this grip on her*" (my italics). This is how I feel! I can't get to my writing because I have no clear moments of authority. The lack of time and energy are real concerns too, but more easily grappled with. This lack of authority is the real obstacle. For days, I tell anyone who will listen about this quote. An artist must have clear moments of authority, I say and know it to be true. "What do you mean,"authority'?" people ask.

It is a bit like confidence, the knowledge that people will listen and respect what you have to say. But it also has to do with being in control, in charge, and comfortable in that position. How is authority earned? Who gives authority? Are we simply trained to bestow it to certain people? Doctors, say, or lawyers, or within the family, to fathers, "the authority figures." I check the dictionary definition and am not surprised to find that authority is linked to the masculine. It is "The accumulated weight of the expressed opinions of the great men of the past. Tradition and authority." How then does the mother/writer garner authority? You can be sure that what she has to say will complicate, if not contradict, the expressed opinions of the "great men of the past." And, without authority, will she speak at all? A tautology, a vicious circle. Without authority, she can't speak and won't be heard, and without speaking she can't be an authority, an author.

In the grocery store, I watch a new mother and her infant waiting in line to return bottles. In five minutes, no less than six people stop to remark about the baby. One woman suggests that baby is too warm, and the mother obligingly unzips the infant's sweater. Another woman approaches the cart and moves the bag of cans away from the baby's hands. The mother, now stacking her cans and bottles on the counter, thanks the woman. The other people only coo at the baby, tell the mother how cute she is. The mother looks a little frazzled by the time her bottles have all been returned, but she smiles or nods at each comment. The baby is not exceptionally beautiful or charming; it is simply a baby, with a clear ribbon of drool on her chin. This unextraordinary child and her mother have unwillingly, perhaps unwantingly, solicited all this attention and scrutiny. Perhaps they enjoy it, see the people's comments and coos as a representation of our feelings of hopefulness, our reverence for the innocence, the possibility in a baby. Or perhaps the mother finds this scrutiny daunting. Perhaps it makes her self-conscious, aware of an audience always gauging her thoughts and behavior. Perhaps she has become uncertain of her words, her authority. Perhaps, like me, she edits every thought before it's complete and can't finish a sentence without questioning it, recasting it, stumbling over words. Like now, for instance, I imagine an audience—impatient, a bit embarrassed for me, thinking of their own mother's talcum-scented bosom, her selfless love. "This essay is idiosyncratic and whiny," the audience chimes. "It's your problem," they say. "The great minds have always operated outside of social norms. If only you were smarter, less sensitive, worked harder. What you need is more focus, more child care."

My own therapist said, in response to this project, "What about Grace Paley? She wrote stories after her children were born. What about Tillie Olsen?" I am thankful for these women writers who found a way to write about the mother's lot, and I don't want to suggest it was easier then—that mother's voices were more welcome in literature or on the Senate floor or in department meetings, because clearly they were not—but different standards apply now to mothering. When I read my daughter the children's books I loved as a child, I'm surprised by what appears by current standards to be negligent parenting—children left in strollers outside the corner grocery or spoken to sternly: "Run along and pick your own berries." We believe that the world is a more dangerous place, and contending with those dangers—real or perceived—is the mother's responsibility. This perception of the world as dangerous and the mother as protector has only increased since Adrienne Rich wrote that the mother is thought to be "the source of angelic love and forgiveness in a world increasingly ruthless and impersonal . . . in a world of wars, brutal competition and contempt for human weakness."

In a recent issue of *Mothering* magazine, Alice Munro, who rarely grants interviews, agreed to speak on the subject of writing and mothering, because "it is important for people like me to say what it's like, give comfort and courage to younger woman." How did she do it? "She put her one-year-old daughter in a playpen and let her four-year-old play with the neighborhood kids." That was forty years ago. Today, manufacturers call playpens "play yards" to distance them from the experts' criticism of them as cages for children. Mothers are cautioned against using them as babysitters:

> Start using the playpen only for emergency duty only, for those times when he needs to be penned in for his own safety or briefly and infrequently for your convenience—while you mop the floor, put something in the oven, answer the phone, go to the bathroom, or straighten up for last minute company. Limit the time he is sentenced to the pen to no more than five to fifteen minutes.

Do I have to be a bad mother to be a writer? How hard it is to completely dismiss those voices when so much is at stake? Annie Dillard writes of the writing life, "your work is so meaningless, so fully for yourself alone, and so worthless to the world, that no one except you cares whether you do it well, or ever." But the opposite might be said for the mothering life. Everything you do is for someone else, and all the world cares how you do it and will hold you responsible for the results. How difficult then, to disengage from one's child to write. For Dillard, her realization is liberating; for the mother it further complicates the situation.

Recently I consulted *What To Expect: The Toddler Years* for help with toilet training and this is what I found:

> Reduce the likelihood of accidents by having your toddler use the potty before leaving the house; by limiting prolonged outings, when possible; by being well-versed in the locations of toilet facilities wherever you go; by stashing an inflatable or regular potty chair in the car trunk . . . or by tucking a foldable potty seat in your tote bag . . . ; by dressing your toddler in easy-off clothes; by watching your toddler carefully for signs of urinary urgency and by suggesting a trip to the toilet at frequent intervals. Avoid (as much as possible) restaurants, stores, homes, and any other destination where floors are covered with expensive carpeting or where the only seating is upholstered.

This is the good mother, the standard to which all others are held up. She is organized, prepared, utterly attuned to her child's needs, self-sacrificing (perhaps she'd like to go to a restaurant or a friend's house, to sink into a large over-stuffed chair?). Barbara

Christian writes of American mothers, "only sacrifice counts as goodness." But can this woman, with her constant vigilance, participate in adult conversation? Can she write? This prescribed vigilance is not only consuming and exhausting; it is, of course, loaded with implied criticism and threat for the mother.

Barely pregnant, I am awarded a fellowship to attend a prestigious writers' conference. I'm nervous, not because of all the famous writers I will meet or the reading I will be required to give, but because I have morning sickness all day long. I want only to sleep, eat saltines, and drink seltzer. When I'm not sleeping, I'm able to hobnob with the bigshot writers, something that has never come easily to me, even when I could have cocktails. Now, of course, I'm not drinking because of the baby. At the time, I thought my confidence was the result of the pregnancy hormones, and perhaps they helped. But now I think my calm derived mostly from the fact that I'd already abandoned my writer self. I could talk easily with the authors because I didn't care anymore. I watched the events as if from some distance, even the workshopping of my story by an author I very much admired. I was, I thought, done with this racket.

But what I couldn't have predicted was the way becoming a mother would deepen and enrich my vision and sensibility. All the daily ministrations of motherhood aren't, as I originally felt them, distractions; they have more fully connected me to this complicated world. The early spring flowers I noticed while pushing my newborn daughter in her stroller were so exquisite, so dazzling, and of such variety and color that I had to learn their names—snow glories, white star of Holland, winter aconite, grape hyacinth. How, I wondered, had I never noticed them before pushing through the sooty snow?

What I'm learning is that writing and mothering needn't be set against each other. They can coexist; they do coexist, as life and art always have. While I read a bedtime story to my daughter, warm and dewy from her bath, I'm thinking of this essay or a story I'm drafting, so that when I reach the end of her book, I can't remember reading the middle of the fairy tale. I am both engaged and idle; I am a mother and a writer.

My daughter has made this all possible, and she has made it all difficult. These statements no longer seem contradictory to me.

133

GIVE ME A SECOND PLEASE . . .

JUSTYNA SEMPRUCH

the background story of a proposal

ZURICH, AUGUST 26, 2003

Just returned from a lecture. Useful advice: If you need to do things you dislike, and especially those you consider a waste of time but you must do them due to some inexplicable sense of responsibility, just do them first, so that they no longer disturb your mind. Clear space for your creativity. Did I hear it right? Great, only that I am sure the person who said that was not a mother, and not even close to becoming one. If I were to follow it, I would never get down to writing. Writing after you have cleared space? Sounds more like a . . . No, I write because I have no choice, and I do it in the middle of the mess. Both in what this mess conceals and in what it points to beyond itself. I am writing in the middle of all that which keeps me from grasping the fact that whatever it is, it never ends. The philosophy of mess. Writing despite the chaos, suspension, incompleteness. Writing as an entry into the law of the father which I, the mother, incorrectly, without clearing the space (for creativity) do, because I need you to read what I have to say and what I try to say but cannot.

*   *   *

VANCOUVER, MARCH 28, 1999

Just realized that Jule is exactly a month old today, and that we spent the whole of March together at home. One month of a particular way of experiencing the world. I must have lost track of time, hopefully not for long, though. Yes, I am beginning to think about my oral exam, the one I missed because the due date did not work out. I would like to go to Europe, back to all the places I knew, and I am reading again, sometimes aloud since I have a listener now.

VANCOUVER, APRIL 12, 1999

I am collecting myself, after the horror of blood, the extracted placenta, and the ambivalence of milk. Listen Jule, it is not easy being mother, but I think it is even harder to be a wife *and* mother. I think I am doing fine as a mother, but the other part is surprisingly unfitting and startlingly incompatible. A grown-up man and a tiny boy competing for my attention. The dominant fantasy of the mother. Am I their fantasy now? A receptacle for the (re)production of sameness? Do they want to keep me enclosed, contained within their desire? Immobilize me in their possession, in the house that is less and less? The experience is negative and authentic. I live in a contradictory society, an upside-down, perverted situation. And yes, I too like Kristeva:

> yearn for the Law. And since it is not made for me alone, I venture to desire outside the law. Then, narcissism thus awakened—the narcissism that wants to be sex—roams, astonished. In sensual rapture I am distraught. Nothing reassures, for only the law sets anything down. Who calls such a suffering jouissance? It is the pleasure of the damned.

VANCOUVER, AUGUST 9, 1999

The little one is into everything now, crawling all over the place. Flower pots are fun, but chewing the phone cable is just the thing. He would love to run, which is funny to look at when you hold him in an upright position and watch his legs impatiently reaching for the ground. His teeth are coming, but he's tough, and so intrigued by the world around him that he tends to forget about the pain. Yesterday we took him for a ride (not a walk), since S. was on his roller blades, and I was following on a bike, while Jule was exhilarated by the sudden acceleration of the matters, contemplating the world and happily chewing on a biscuit until he dropped it out of excitement.

Jule woke up and fell off the bed. The fall—his first vehicle, a chute, really, for the defense of his own identity. I am no longer upset that we live in a carpeted apartment. Still, I have to examine his tiny body to make sure that his crying is due just to the shock of the fall. It is not the first time though, and we bought him a baby cot but he refuses to sleep there. He insists on sleeping with his hand buried in my hair. I cut my hair short, but it makes no difference. A dialectical experience in its essence. Negation of togetherness which stubbornly returns to confirm itself. Here it comes, the upside down experi-

135

ence which takes the immediate form of nausea, shock, alienation, and despair. Here he comes, happily crawling again, heading for the paper basket. And the basket is full. Full of my unfinished thoughts, full of attempts, hopes, and desires.

AUGUST 18, 1999

You are asking me if I have time to write. Well, I don't. My life has shrunk into the size of a baby world. Everything revolves around Jule. In the morning I still think that I could do so much, but then all the other things are coming, and I need to hold on, I need to ignore the brain, as if I were ignoring the full bladder, pretending that it gives me no pain. And then the day is over, and I look at a book on the table, and just as I am about to reach for it, I decide to clear the mess. Julian's stuff has dominated the entire place. There is an abyss between me and my writing, and I refer to Kristeva again:

> then there is this other abyss that opens up between the body and what had been its inside: there is the abyss between the mother and the child. What connection is there between myself, or even more unassumingly between my body and this internal graft and fold, which, once the umbilical cord has been severed, is an inaccessible other?

I am a continuous separation, a division of flesh and language. But what's even worse is, I don't have enough money.

*   *   *

ZURICH, MAY 08, 2003

Hard to begin. After a long silence. The silence has become my outer representation. Not in my head, though. Believe me, my head is exploding. With fragments of proposals, assignments, and abstracts. I may signify a silent ground, a scarcely representable mystery, but at least I am a plenum. Of course, you encounter opacity and resistance in me—menacing traces of the father's phallus—but I, at least, am not nothing. To paraphrase Irigaray I am not that vacuum [of] woman.

My child is constantly talking to me. Now, as he learns to speak, he is talking back. And I am slowly recognizing all the different words and phrases I have been using over the last couple of years. In different languages.

ZURICH, MAY 17, 2003

Between Private Emotions and the Social Order: A Preliminary Proposal for a Project on Parenthood

It is often believed that we are living in a postfeminist time. This claim, partly due to the exaggerated focus on women who have "made it," is highly theoretical, if not misleading, no matter whether we assume that their career is tokenism or a success. My

136

proposal for a study results from what I have observed during my doctoral studies in Canada and in the last three years of my life in Switzerland. Whereas in Canada . . .

Mama?

Just a second, Jule . . . Whereas in Canada . . .

Can we go for a walk?

Just a . . .

Let's go for a short walk

Jule, please . . .

Mama, please . . .

ZURICH, AUGUST 16, 2003

137

Trying to concentrate, attempting to focus on one of the unfinished papers. Collecting ideas never put down. What was I doing all the time? Taking care of the boy? Even though "I have a nanny," (I am quoting my husband). "I have a nanny." Can you imagine? Not for Jule, but I am the one in need of a nanny. Why? Because I am not a full mother. I am a part-timer. An occasional mother.

My standpoint is . . . mama—wait a second, Jule, I'm in the middle of a sentence—my standpoint is that no matter how we define family, or those who might serve to represent it, (anyway, who should be empowered to decide any of these questions?) those of us who for various reasons "have become" parents inevitably enter a socio-juridical system of "parenthood" in which carefully constructed (read: patriarchal) roles are still being practiced, played and replayed "for the sake of our children." It is the socio-philosophical aspect of parenthood, often wrongly reduced to motherhood and dooming the "mother" to some "instinct-driven" sacrifices and obligations that I attempt to explore in my study. In other words, caring (for dependents) has its costs and benefits, but are they equally distributed in a/the family understood foremost as an institutionally sanctioned heterosexual couple?

Are you done with your sentence?

My boy is four and a half, thinking and acting quite independently, but coming back to me, making sure that I am present. What if he were not? I would have written two books or more, but I would not have written him. I would not have responded to a tiny human being, but to a thought or a concept, to a desire without shape and body, not a mind and a mouth to feed.

He is the one who keeps me here, incapable of planning my independence, reducing my traveling to dreaming, incapable of packing a suitcase if I wish to. And I do have a wish like that, a room of my own. There I am sitting and writing and contemplating feminisms. The wish is buried under the stack of unfinished projects, projects-to-be. Perhaps I will finish them when Jule gets older, but won't I get old too?

Look Mama, look, he says, spreading a road map on the floor. *Here is a car driving, and here is a train station, and this is where dada works.* I am getting curious, now. *Yeah? Is this his office?* He looks at me, then at the map. *Right here, next to the bus stop. And where do I work, Julian?* I ask. I truly wonder what he will say, since my place of work is an abstract.

Let's go, Mama, I am ready to go . . .

My work has no place assigned to it, and still it consumes my days entirely, the days of being with Jule, the days when "daddy" is providing for us, (I am quoting again), it is mainly, principally, and predominantly his money that we live on—we have a sugar daddy. My work? I work for a little extra money that I get from teaching. Just enough not to be able to think about it and it is gone already, so here I am, present but not available, always in front of my laptop, not even *my* laptop, but borrowed from daddy, or otherwise, running to my classes, teaching on an hourly basis, and then off to conferences (sponsored by daddy). But the sponsorship has its downfalls. I hear a lot about the extra costs I am causing. And then I am back home, writing, reading, thinking.

Mama, why are you reading all the time?

It's Jule, carrying a stack of books under his arm to take a seat next to me, and to read by himself. Although he cannot read yet, he spends lots of time sitting right next to me, his left foot touching my hip.

So where is my place of work, Julian? He hesitates, I can clearly see that. *Your work . . . is not on the map,* and then he adds, convincing himself, (and me): *it is on the outside, you know?*

How convenient—my work is on the outside, not a normal type of job, no office, no regular working hours, no time appointments, no after-work parties. My work is to write anywhere I can, as much as I can, under different circumstances, and to remind you about the perverted world. To go beyond the antagonisms of the dialectic and to hold down a job on the side—to be a housewife, and a good mother, and smooth lover (and I am lucky because no perfection is expected). I am desperate because I thought I could leap over the last one. But no, the last one is too hard for me. It is easier to move from one country to another, and when I am not sure in which language, I should cross the border and invent the language. Yes, I can do that. Invent things to avoid the vacuum of the outside. But I cannot face up to my life where it is most painful and where its pretense becomes obvious.

ZURICH, AUGUST 22, 2003

But today, I am fine. Julian is with the nanny, one of those brave women you seldom hear about, unless something goes wrong. One whose name should be included in the acknowledgments of my dissertation. One of those ambiguous women, a Polish nanny with a status of a visitor in the country where everything seems to work so much better. Hoping for a miracle.

Writing about my child is writing about the nanny. Our nanny. She is reflected in my child's body, his language, and his memory. I am reflected in her. I can hear them now, coming back from the playground. Swiss playgrounds are full of kids and their nannies; playgrounds are their meeting points. This is where they smoke, exchange stories and complain about women like me. Playgrounds are where they compare their wages, their living conditions; playgrounds are where I go occasionally and where nobody knows me.

So you are Julian's mother; nice to meet you; good to see you; Julian is a sunny boy. Do you want to hear about a sunny boy?

Sunshine, Mama, if there is sunshine here, is it dark in Canada? When are you coming back? Very soon Julian, just a few of your sunshines and I am back.

Today, I am at home, just about to check my e-mail. *Mama, where are you? Are you here?* His first steps are towards my bedroom, where I work since we have our nanny—she lives in the office. My office room, tax-deductible, goes to the nanny. It's an office and a library and a guest room. But, in fact, it's a refuge, a sanctuary of ideas and possibilities, filed and ordered in stacks, with a little extra space for a visitor, unaware of the particular order of things hastily pushed under the bed. It is also a space for speculation, but not decorative, ornamental speculation, but a space for a non-hierarchical insight. An insight into my inside, my other pregnancy.

Julian likes to bring his books into that room with all the tiny cars and trains, parked alongside the hard covers. He opens one of the books and says, *Mama, I want you to have a big stomach, like this. Let's have another baby.* No, Julian, I am too busy, daddy is too busy, I need to work, I need to find a job, a good tenured position. I need money, not babies. I cannot live on daddy's money, it doesn't work.

But maybe I can. Maybe I have masochistic tendencies, living with a man and a boy and another woman, of whom no one is my lover. There is some obligation, some sweetness, some leveraging of power. But pleasure of being is not there.

Mama, you are my life.

Mama, what is life?

I am writing against stagnation of mind, against laziness that overcomes you when you're stuck in the repetitive care taking tasks. I am writing against the necessity to pick up and clean everything after the baby. I am also writing against marriage, against heterosexuality, against obligations. Of? Of reference: Yes, my husband has a well paid job, it keeps us going; yes, I stay at home with our child sometimes. No I am not employed. I am writing against this type of life that many would be jealous of, if they only knew what I know.

What do I know? I know what pleasure is and what pleasure is not. Counting words. How much more should I include? I have said nothing yet. To paraphrase Irigaray: given that the first body I had any dealing with was a woman's body, and that the first love I shared was her love, I, unlike S., stand in an archaic and primal relationship with what is known as homosexuality.

And you, Julian? Coming out of my womb, the "first house to surround you," will you think of it no more? Will it be nothing but waste to be disposed of if you translate it into language? And how will you forget this "openness that is threatening, that unleashes the danger of pollution," and that is sweet and that you will crave for in many of your dreams to come? Or, is it contamination and "engulfment in illness, madness, and death."

Mhhhh . . . no more. Shut down the computer, Mama, stop writing. I don't want to listen to it any more, my ears hurt.

Just give me a second, Jule. There is still something I have been meaning to tell you. *Yeah? What is it then?*

Come on, it's a secret. I will whisper it into your ears:

....*wow!*

Shhhhhhhhhhhhhhhhhhhhhhhhhhh, can you keep a secret?

Sure.

Then, we say no more.

Where are we going then, mama?

We—yes, of course, we are going to—wait, Jule. Till I finish this proposal so that I, so that we can get the grant, really soon. It's a promise. And then we'll cross the big waters one more time.

STONES AND SPOONS

BETH LUCHT

SHE CHECKED their tiny, sleeping bodies, left out bread and milk, cracked the window, stuffed towels beneath the door to the room, and taped the edges. Then she crept downstairs, took a bottle-full of pills, laid her head on the oven door, and waited to die.

When she heard the news, her friend Anne Sexton (who would be dead by her own hand eleven years later) wrote:

> O Sylvia, Sylvia,
> with a dead box of stones and spoons,
> with two children, two meteors
> wandering loose in a tiny playroom,
> with your mouth into the sheet,
> into the roofbeam, into the dumb prayer,
> (Sylvia, Sylvia
> where did you go
> after you wrote me
> from Devonshire
> about raising potatoes
> and keeping bees?)

what did you stand by,
just how did you lie down into?

I cannot help but be angry when I think of the tiny bodies and the bread and milk laid out in the chilly English flat. Sylvia Plath, sainted as a victim, a tortured soul who nevertheless had the mother's sense to set out food for her babies nevertheless left her babies, alone and abandoned. Nicholas and Frieda were discovered, cold and frightened in their room, by the visiting nurse who had broken into the house and found Plath's body.

Frieda, a poet and painter herself, wrote of the women who worshiped her mother: "Wanting to breathe life into their own dead babies/ They took her dreams, collected words from one/ Who did their suffering for them."

Suffering for us, she was abandoned by a philandering husband and left alone with two small children to face the harshest English winter in sixty years. Ted Hughes, later the poet laureate of England, spent that winter in sunny Spain with his mistress. Six years later, that woman, Assia Wevill, would also stick her head in the oven and die, joined by Shura, the two-year-old daughter she and Hughes had together. I do not know much of Wevill's story, though I do know she was tormented by the empty space left behind by Plath, and by Hughes' guilty remembrances.

Looking for instruction and guidance on how to be both a writer and a mother, I find death instead. I find Plath, of course, and also her friend, Anne Sexton. Sexton is rumored to have made snacks for her children before taking her own life, prompting one woman on a website I visited to comment, "What a mother!" I find the poet Reetika Vazirani, who killed herself and her two-year-old son in July of 2003, distraught over her failing marriage.

I am angry with these women, and conflicted about my anger. I understand why I am angrier with Plath than I am at John Berryman, who threw himself in the Mississippi River, leaving behind three daughters, the youngest only an infant. I am angrier because Plath was a mother, and I am a mother, and somehow in my mind, mothers have more of a duty to stick around. That's not very feminist of me, though I am also angry at Kurt Cobain for leaving behind his then-tiny daughter; the only time I've liked Courtney Love was when she was outside with his fans the night after his death, waving his suicide note around and yelling, "Asshole! Asshole!"

I'm also confused about my anger because I know that Plath and Sexton weren't victims, they weren't emblems—they were ill. Both women suffered from mental illness and had struggled for years before they succumbed. I work in an emergency mental health unit and I talk every day with people who are feeling suicidal. I know the statistics: 10 percent of people with schizophrenia will die by suicide, 19 percent of those with bipolar illness will take their own lives, and about 15 percent of individuals with a major depression diagnosis will kill themselves. Just as I don't blame my clients for having an illness, I should not blame them when they kill themselves. But I do. I see the wreckage they leave behind. I cast my blame most vociferously when I see children left behind by their mother, the one person in the world most charged with protecting them.

The fact that I look for mothers who write (or writers who mother) and I find dead madwoman should be no surprise. Studies of artists over the years have found two to

142

three times the prevalence of substance abuse, affective disorders, psychosis, and suicide attempts than is found in the general population. Even supposedly "healthy" creative people have traits that are often commonly found in people with mental illness.
Researchers at Stanford looked at a group of mentally healthy writers and artists and
found that, compared to a control group of non-artists, they were more likely to be
impulsive, anxious, aloof, and hostile, as well as being independent, nonconformist, and
open to new experiences.

I don't write very much or very well when I'm stable. I can manage nonfiction or
essays, but trying to get poems to come is hopeless. They flow like water when my world
is falling apart; five years ago, with my marriage crumbling, I had a poem come to me
every time I crossed the room. I scribbled incessantly, spent my days attending to that
hazy inner-world of words and rhythms and sudden, alarming metaphors, and even won
a hotshot local poetry prize. Since then, nothing. I wonder if I have to fall apart, lose my
job, kick my boyfriend out, fall in love with someone else, or worse, to write again in the
possessed way I did before. Some days I think it might be worth it, but then I remember:
I'm a mother.

My job is to be regular and constant, to get dinner on the table by a reasonable hour,
to not allow the pile of dirty dishes in the sink to become perilously high. All dreams of
artistic glory aside, I can't shirk what I see as my duty. I have to find the little cracks of
danger and wildness between the steppingstones of normal, prosaic family life. It's really hard, and most of the time I can't do it.

When I did an Internet search with several combinations of terms designed to bring
up information about poets who were (living) mothers, I didn't find much. I found a large
number of references to male poets who have written about their mothers, but not much
about mamas who write. I did find a little interview with two Boston mothers, neither of
whom I have ever heard of, but both of who said things that resonate with me. Linda
Haviland Conte, when asked about how she manages to write and mother, commented,
"It is difficult to have children and have a serious intellectual pursuit." I couldn't agree
more. I'm done with liberating myself by celebrating the one-in-a-million who manages
to write the next Great American Novel on her laptop while pushing a grocery cart or
baby carriage. I want to make myself feel better by bitching about how hard it is. Of
course, it's not just the kids that dull your brain, it's lack of sleep and the dreary day-job
and the nodding out in front of the television and the needing to fold the laundry that's
been sitting in the corner for two weeks. In general, it is probably very hard to have a
serious intellectual pursuit as an adult in this world unless you are one of the lucky people who are paid to have such.

That idea that would probably offend Wallace Stevens, who was vice president of
the Hartford Accident and Indemnity Company and on his walks to work, wrote some of
the most important and celebrated poems of the twentieth century. He didn't have a
problem finding freedom and imagination between the bricks of his staid life. I also
know that there was a Mrs. Stevens who did the worrying about the basket of laundry in
the corner, so that Mr. Stevens could have more brain-space to devote to metaphor and
imagery and finding the perfect word.

143

Even if my brain worked well enough, I don't know if I could write as much as I want to. The other Boston poet I mentioned, Joanne Holdridge, references my other great problem: "The hardest thing about kids is the lack of solitude, the constant interruptions." It's not just the kids, it's the world. In my house, if it isn't my son, it's my boyfriend, or the telephone, or the sudden seductive call of e-mail. In a wired world, you are never truly alone. Sometimes I am even interrupted by an absolutely desperate need to sweep the kitchen or scrub the toilet. The problem, for me, is the intrusion of real life and its necessities, combined with the incredible lengths to which I, like many writers, will go in order to avoid actually writing. Holdridge also issues a reminder, which I would be well to heed, saying, "Poetry helps parenting because it's about pausing and seeing. Having a child makes it very hard to pause and see when they are always with you."

I think pausing and seeing not only help parenting, they also help life. I'm not much for pausing in most situations. I plunge ahead, dispatching tasks with a sometimes-savage efficiency. I am not about being in the moment; I am about lists and plans. I fear the moment—what if I got caught in the moment and I couldn't get out? This is undoubtedly what keeps poetry trapped within me. I keep moving forward, propelled by a fear of falling apart if I stop, and a creaking, nagging phobia of getting too much one-on-one time with myself.

So I fear lapsing into the moment, worried that it will sap my ability to produce and to parent, but then sometimes it occurs to me, just like the poet from Boston says, being able to just *be* is a parenting skill too, one at least as important as the ability to multitask, but one rarely practiced by most parents. We are so busy scheduling our children and shuffling them around that we rarely just sit and do whatever it is that the child wants. (Family therapists actually call this kind of doing whatever "special play," and teach it to troubled families, like just sitting around and goofing off is a special skill you need an advanced degree to explain.) You're not going to get trapped just being in the moment forever with your kid, because eventually the kid's going to get hungry or thirsty or need to go to the bathroom. Come to think of it, we adults have those bodily needs too (though we're better at repressing them) and eventually, they do pull us back to earth.

A while ago, my son came home from his father's. Some days, he's all boy, but on this day, he seemed to be playing the role of the daughter I always wanted. We spent half an hour crocheting, and he talked at length about his plans to make dolls that look like superhero versions of our cats. (At school, he writes constantly about them under their stage names, Super Minna and Super Louis, and they've become cult heroes of a sort.) He read aloud to me from a Little House book. After dinner, we cleared off the table and brought out some egg cartons, potting soil, and seeds so he could plant some flowers.

Helping him stick seeds in the dirt and chatting about how tall each plant would eventually grow, I felt like I was the mom I had wanted to be. For years, I've been dragging him outside to garden, and mostly trying to snatch a little surreptitious weeding or planting while he was briefly distracted by his ongoing project to hit everything he can with a stick. But this is the way I'd always thought it would be—aiming ourselves at a common project, him asking me for guidance while doing his own thing, too.

When I let go of my need to *do* for long enough to really roll up my sleeves and *be*, I realized that he could serve as my role model. His imagination lets him move into rooms that I don't acknowledge, so long have they been boarded up. His lyrics would put many a surrealistically oriented songwriter to shame. (An excerpt from my recent favorite: "There's only one nun left in the world/But she's a ton of help/With the shack and the sacks/We use to hold the thumbtacks.") I've realized that my goal as a mother and my goal as an artist can be the same, at least some of the time: I need to spend less time trying to make my child stop acting like a child, and work harder to spend more time being like a child myself. There still has to be an adult in the relationship, one who pays the utility bills and insists that we can't just have ice cream sundaes for dinner, but I need a daily vacation from being that person. It deadens me to spend all day, every day, inhabiting that role.

Maybe, in addition to untreated illness, there was something else that killed Plath: the feeling that her writer-self and her mother-self were mutually exclusive. Some people still to this day think they were. Witness a post I found on the Sylvia Plath forum:

> "Her poetry has proved to every woman and man that giving birth does transform the woman into something less superior. The woman's mind becomes soggy and empty. Sylvia had a great mind that crumbled into fragments because of the domesticated environment (sic) that she lived in. Here was a great mind that was put to chopping vegetables (sic) and cleaning floors. This is why Sylvia Plath might of (sic) put an end to this situation. Even though a love for her children was very present it wasn't enough to keep her alive.

Plath did continue to write up until her death, sometimes rising at 4:00 A.M. to write, as she said, in "that still blue, almost eternal hour before the baby's cry, before the glassy music of the milkman, settling his bottles." The poems that she left behind prove that her mind was not rotted past the point of no return by chopping vegetables, but she herself may not have believed it. The battle between her selves, and the difficulty of melding a synthesis of them, may have been too much.

Surely some days my mind is soggy and empty, just as it was on some days before I became a parent. I know that mothering locks me out from some places that I want to go. It also opens doors I never would have seen had I not become a mother. I've accepted being a little unhappy in each of my selves sometimes, which isn't *good* but it's better than being miserable in any one spot. The pull between disparate goals and modes of being is a fundamental piece of who I am; if I was well-integrated and satisfied all the time, I probably wouldn't recognize myself. But I think I'm on the path. No matter how slowly I progress, I need to remember that it's worth staying on the trip, and that the trip isn't about the end anyway, it's about the journey. The journey is looking into that seven-year-old face which will never again see the world the same way as he does today, and remembering: slow down and see. Be here with this person, be here in this place. Be here and be pleased to be here. And maybe, if I slow down enough, all that being and seeing may come out in a poem, a poem not rooted in despair or desperation, but one which might even have a little to do with joy, and grows from the fullness of my life.

COLLABORATION

HEATHER CUSHMAN-DOWDEE

ONCE UPON a time, a few years back, my Inspired Husband and I decided that we should continue our plans and attend graduate school for visual arts. A decision that by most standards was chock-full of crazy because I was a new and lactating mama. Yet, full of trepidation, we attended our orientation with our Tiny Daughter in a sling. And, after that, she was at school with us all day, every day. Why did no one on the faculty ever question her presence? Insightful Husband is sure that the faculty just assumed someone else had given us approval. Who can say, but for most of the three years of our graduate degree she was the sole child on campus.

In the beginning, our day would go something like this: I scooped Excited Daughter up into the sling and walked her to the door of our spacious 10' x 12' studio where we waved goodbye to Sculptor Husband as he walked to his own work space. Our space was outfitted with shelves for art supplies, a couch for naps, and a sandbox on the floor. (Concerned Husband thought I was crazy for this bit of indulgence, but us mamas will do anything for quiet and peace of mind.) Other than the sandbox, there wasn't a toy in the space. Not one. And she never missed them. I would set to work on my first project: a series of large paintings with breastfeeding, specifically the weightlessness of babies, as subject matter. I worked from a stepladder to keep the bottoms of the paintings just out of Stretchable Daughter's creative reach, although it always seemed necessary to incorporate scribbles into the bottom of my work. In exchange for a glorious hour or two of

painting, I would give her free rein to create her own work (which she did, she did!). I called it: Studio Installation, Rhapsody in Blue. To the untrained eye, a blue scribble that covered and encircled the entire bottom of the studio, including the shelves, couch, stepladder, carpet, sandbox, and a few times even my legs. The sandbox became less a place for sand play and more the staging and mixing area for Artistic Daughter's work. Brand new bottles of paint were poured out into the box and mixed to stiff consistency with the sand and glitter and whatnot, and then spackled to surfaces.

Each day we would walk to the library across the campus where Rambunctious Daughter would careen up and down the aisles, squealing with delight, mixing it up in her own wacky way. Or we would go to the Art Supply store, where I would tell Greedy Daughter that she could pick out *"two* things," but in the end I would relent and buy her four, because she might *really need* that green tempera, that glo-pen, that silver glitter *and* the gorilla stickers. Who am I to stand in the way of inspiration? And then we would return to the studio in time for Fatigued Daughter's nap. After breastfeeding her off to sleep, I would hastily begin painting again. I was not allowed the luxury of thought processes, which in my pre-child day involved endless staring, long drags of a cigarette, and the occasional dab of a new color. Then the entire process would be repeated and repeated with the alternate versions being: listening to music while smoking and occasionally dabbing the paint, or talking with other artists in long meandering conversa-

COLLABORATION: *Heather Cushman-Dowdee*

tions while smoking and occasionally dabbing the paint. But those were my pre-child days. In graduate school, I contemptuously called those thought processes "contemplating the belly button." I didn't have time anymore. Every minute for creative pursuits takes on urgency when your time is shared with a little one. I would make all my creative decisions—color, composition, style—while breastfeeding, walking, playing, and eating outside of the studio, and then as soon as a moment to paint was presented, I learned to seize it and paint, paint, paint. It's the number one rule of mothering, I guess. Seize the day! Seize the moment! Mama doesn't have time for endless considerations, and you know what? —my output since Inspiring Daughter came along has been prolific.

By the end of that first semester, Intrepid Daughter could walk her grandparents across campus to the student union, showing them the way. She had her very own pair of safety goggles so that she could help her Inventive Daddy in the woodshop and she was on a first name-basis with a good portion of the faculty. Sweet Daughter's hair and skin obtained a constant griminess and a tinge of blue that gave her a highly bohemian look.

My Artist Daughter was not yet two.

That summer, Innovative Husband and I finagled a way to travel to Europe and gain independent study credit (a huge perk of being enrolled at a university). Packing our entire family into one backpack, and taking along the first stroller we had ever used, we went to visit five countries by train in two months. Everyone told us that we were crazy to attempt this, as Terrific Daughter had just turned two. Would we listen to their opinion? That, to put it bluntly, two can be terrible? Well, the opinions of others are generally the litmus for us to do just the opposite. So we went, and it wasn't so very terrible. Except it was impossible to spend long hours luxuriously people-watching in cafés. Endearing Daughter would smile sweetly and play and chat until the drinks were served and then "She's Off!" would bolt across the busy city square. Every time. I would make chase (which is the worst way to get a toddler to come back), all the while yelling at her racing back, "I raised you as a 'continuum concept' child, you aren't supposed to run away!" We had to get used to the forced march of traveling with a toddler. Inventive Husband and I were supposed to be working on an artistic project, but instead we were spending all of our time pushing Demanding Daughter around in the stroller—a stroller that she perceived to be like a prison; her sentence was staring at the kneecaps of tourists in ill-advised shorts. We couldn't stop. Oh no, if we stopped, Exuberant Daughter wanted to run, so we walked. And walked. And walked. By Intrepid Husband's estimates (he's not prone to exaggeration) we walked more than ten miles a day. After Exhausted Daughter went to bed in the hotel, we would crouch cross-legged on the floor, toss back bottles of wine, and whisper furtively the plans for our project.

This is the project: We arranged to have posters of our art plastered all over the city of Amsterdam for two weeks in a project we called "Creating Celebrity." See how we accommodated Despotic Daughter? We picked Amsterdam, a truly kid-friendly city, because it is decidedly anti-automobile. We rented bikes, and safely ensconced her on the back. No more forced march, no more parenting trail of tears, just the wind in Relieved Daughter's hair and the view whizzing by. We biked to each of the locations and photographed the posters all over the city. Her job was to yell, "There's mommy and daddy" whenever she saw a poster and we would mark them "found" on the map.

Amsterdam was also perfect, because of its combination of accessible french fries, big grassy parks, and a truly wonderful invention: the combination café-playground.

For all of our accommodation though, Worldly Daughter seemed genuinely relieved to come home so that she could get back to work on her art.

And me, too.

I began to create a character called Hathor the Cowgoddess, and a new project named *Hathor's Kitchen*. Hathor's first appearance was to be as a baker of breastmilk bread in a kitchen/temple at an on-campus gallery. The project consisted of cartoon paintings, flour bags, rising dough, and just-baked bread shaped as breasts and piled high in two breast-like mounds. I appeared as Hathor for two hours a day during Reliable Daughter's naptime, but she was as likely to be there too. She would stand at the table, kneading bread with a surety that most of the college students who I invited to help, lacked. I must say that my Naive Daughter became proficient at kneading dough and shaping it into breast shapes with a wee dab of egg to make the nipple shiny. Not generally a skill she would learn in pre-school. This skill still causes stares when she practices with sand at playgrounds.

Our days leading up to this project were filled with scouring second-hand stores for tablecloths, towels, bowls, spoons; painting in the studio; and teaching a freshman drawing class. Intent Daughter would sit at an easel, clutching her charcoal and pencil along with all of the other students. So many of these college students would timidly tell me that they "can't draw," and "don't know how to draw," until I wondered what ever happened to them. My Engrossed Daughter would size up the naked model in the center of the room and begin with a scribble that confidently covered the page. She was just about three years old.

There were times when we were in school together that I would have said that Youthful Daughter was many years older than her true age. Responsible, sensible, creative—she could cut with sharp grown-up scissors, though only two. Whenever I painted with large strokes on giant canvases, her rhythm would become more peaceful, more concentrated, and when I sculpted, she built and stacked and glued and found her own pace as well. I spent great gobs of time agonizing over the materials I used, to accommodate having her small body in the studio with me. Oil paints were out of the question, so I switched to acrylic for the ease of skin clean-up. I chose Sculpey over traditional clay so that I could be interrupted and not freak out. I chose glitter because Trendy Daughter thought it was cool. Her small body determined why I began to use bread in my work, why we did a poster project by bike in Amsterdam, and why I created Hathor the Cowgoddess. Ultimately, she is the reason for everything I do.

Our third year of school was spent in preparation for our thesis show, which would be shown in the Contemporary Art Museum, and at some venues in other cities. My part of the production was a series of large black and white and glitter cartoon drawings, painted and quilted protest banners, and small tchotchke-style sculptures of Hathor the Cowgoddess. Artist Daughter's work was to be shown underneath and around the walls, like a watermark, like a finished version of the studio installation she had been working diligently for three years.

As I began to cull Profuse Daughter's best pieces from the massive pile we had collected, I used one criterion to include it in the show: the work must be entirely her own. How easy to fulfill the requirement; she rarely had anyone tell her what to draw. No one corrected or urged or enhanced her drawings. She was on her own to do what she wanted—to paint, explore, mess up, and destroy as much or as little as she wanted. In the beginning, it was a trade-off for peace of mind, so that I could get my own work done. But then, as she blossomed into a hugely creative, intelligent toddler, the trade-off became a conscious decision, a lifestyle choice. Who am I to say what makes something beautiful? Why would she need me to tell her how to draw a tree? Given the materials, the space, and the time, can't we all create masterpieces? Even the two-year-olds among us? And deep down, isn't that everyone's ultimate goal: finding the materials, the time, and the space to follow our dreams? Sure, I sometimes worried that my lack of direction and Unruly Daughter's utter abandon bordered on negligence. "Shouldn't I be designing cute craft projects and hovering over her shoulder?" I would wonder. But I didn't cave. I abandoned hovering when I entered graduate school and began to follow my own dreams and work on my own work, and as a consequence, her finished drawings were staggeringly beautiful (they still are). And they were/are her very own. Of course, as Mama I am a bit prejudiced—maybe they aren't the masterpieces of my mental-making. But really, who is the judge? And if I believe it to be true, doesn't that make it so?

In those days at school, I learned so many things, many of which were taught by Enlightened Daughter: how to truly let go and be creative, how to love unconsciously, to play diligently, and work effortlessly. All good lessons, surely. But one of the best things she taught me is to collaborate. To share my time and energy, but not to smother or hover. To work alongside, but not through. To walk the same path, but to have separate goals. Our best qualities flowered in that 10' x 12' studio space, and grew as Independent Daughter worked alongside Occupied Mama, each creatively following her own dreams. And, to this day, I look beside me, and wow, there she is doing her own work, too.

HOW TO MAKE
A RECORD LABEL

EILEEN ALDEN

1. late at night, when the kids are finally asleep, at least temporarily, re-charge your creative energy. find a sitter to come over while you sneak out near midnight, wearing sneakers and comfortable clothes. go to an underground deep house party and take some time when you first walk in to let the rhythm and chords fill you with positivity. settle in and get comfortable as you start to shed your worries about the kids and the bills and all your responsibilities and you forget the world outside the club. then as the loud soulful house music kicks in and takes control of your body and mind, let yourself go and dance into oblivion with a room full of sweaty, ecstatic humans waving their hands in the air and celebrating life. come home exhausted but rejuvenated. dream wonderful thoughts of spreading your music to make people dance all over the world because it's your passion*.

2. in the morning, after coffee, realize that in order to fulfill your dream you will need to make some 12" records for djs to spin. (there are other ways to do it, but this is the coolest.) 12" records are the same old vinyl format that djs have been spinning for years, sometimes a single song with multiple versions, or sometimes it's a 1-4 song "ep" with different songs from one or more artists.

3.   learn how to make tracks yourself, or find a partner to work with who makes tracks, or find artists you like who make tracks. tracks are the songs on a 12" record. some labels find people who are selling a lot of records and ask them to do original tracks or remixes. remixes are just reinterpretations of an original song. it's great to have remixes or songs from a big name producer, but make sure these tracks are really your sound and something that you love, not just a top seller, or else your label will become generic and just another paycheck for dj big kahuna. you may have to pay a lot for tracks and remixes from established artists, but if you deal with up-and-coming artists, especially people you know, you can usually pay them next to nothing up-front, and give them a cut of the profits after the record sells.

4.   convince the artist that the tracks you like best are really done (if, in fact, the tracks are actually done to your satisfaction). It can be hard to get any artist to consider their work "complete," but if the artist doesn't finish it, you will never have anything to release.

153

5.   try to play the tracks out at a club to see how they sound on a big system. ask your close dj friends to drop them in a set, or play them yourself if you are a dj. if there's something wrong with the mix, try to fix it. the mix is the final balance between the instruments and sounds. sometimes you may find one instrument too loud, etc., and you need to rework it.

6.   take the track to a studio where they record tracks that go onto vinyl (if possible), or to someone who's been in the business of making tracks for club play for a while, and get the tracks "premastered" which means they basically fine-tune the overall sound. this is a really important step a lot of people miss, or try to do it themselves using software. but to get the best results, it helps to have another set of ears involved, preferably someone with experience, especially on the first few releases.

7.   get a friend (or try it yourself if you know art-design software programs) to design a center label for you, using templates available online from one of the pressing plants. the pressing plants are the manufacturing shops that actually create the records.

8.   don't make full-color jackets until your label is established; they cost too much money and you won't break even. it's much more cost effective to use colorful center labels and plain black or white jackets.

8. (a).   if you do decide to blow some money on jacket art, this adds another artistic dimension—deciding on the graphic design. The design and manufacturing of the jackets is a big subject, worthy of a lengthy discussion on its own. but, ultimately, it is inevitable: you will contemplate putting your kid's photo on the jacket. cute kid doing some cute kid activity such as eating ice cream, cute kid staged to look like a grown-up, blown-up photo of a kid's cute face, etc. so before taking this step, at least consider the pros and cons:

1. pro: it's virtually free.

2. pro: it would be totally clever and eye-catching.

3. pro: your kid might become famous in the house music scene, and will thank you for the rest of her life for being such a cool mom.

4. con: your opinion of the photos of your kid is totally subjective and naturally biased, so other people might actually think the picture is cheesy.

5. con: your kid has completely different taste in music, and will actually hate being associated with the record.

6. con: the house music label is at least one part of your life where you can stop being a total mom for a goddamn minute. so if you're going to invest in getting some color jackets made, let it be your own artistic expression, whatever that may be, because this is the time and the place for it.

9.   pick a record pressing plant such as RTI or music connection (the old WEA plant). there are only a handful of record pressing plants in the U.S., and you can find them online or look at some records you like, to see where they were made. fill out an account opening form with them, and send them your artwork. keep in mind, they will expect payment before they send you your records, usually some up front and some when the tests are approved. this will be important when we get to 'distributors.' don't make more than 1,000 records of your first release. you can always make more, but you can't eat them if they don't sell (i have heard that you can make them into bowls but i've never tried that....)

10.   make sure you also request one hundred or so promo copies which should be sent to you with plain white labels, and you should have them shipped to you to arrive around three weeks before the release date. these are the records you will use to promote your record; they are the advance copies that will be circulated before the release actually comes out.

11.   get your premastered audio turned into a lacquer master by a pro in the business**. almost all of the "mastering guys" in this country, who have experience cutting lacquer masters and are still doing it, are located in New York and L.A. it's really important to pick someone good to cut your record, someone considered an expert in your genre, especially when you're just starting out. if you pick someone who doesn't like dance music, for example, and used to cut regular rock and roll records in the 70s, the record won't play well in a club, because it won't have enough low end. you can look up the mastering credit on house records you like, and try to find someone you can work with. don't bother trying to get a sample of what the lacquer masters sound like after they've been cut—it's impossible because they can't actually make you a copy. just trust them. if you insist on getting a sample version of their lacquer master, they will very often charge you close to the full price, anyway. this is because each time they create a lacquer master, they are actually using a lathe to carve a piece of lacquer; there is no way to just make a copy of it. to make an extra copy actually entails going through the carving process a second time, and no two carvings will be exactly identical.

12. the mastering guy will send the lacquer masters direct to the pressing plant immediately after he cuts them, and the lacquers will start to deteriorate (i.e. melt) soon after they are made, so it's very important your account is open and you are squared away with the pressing plant BEFORE you get the lacquers cut.

13. the pressing plant will take the lacquers and make plates out of them. the plates are like molds and are used to physically press the records. after they do the plating, they will send you test presses (usually three to five). the purpose of these is to make sure that nothing screwed-up in the process during the making of the lacquers or plates.

14. take your test presses and listen carefully to several of them. make sure there are no weird pops or scratches or other noises that shouldn't be there. make sure the sound quality is good (at least as good as the premastered version). if possible, play it out at a club or ask one of your dj friends to play it. go to the club when he or she plays it and scream a lot when you hear it come on. buy the dj some drinks.

15. if it sounds ok, send the pressing plant your approval and the rest of the payment and wait for your promos (the white label copies you ordered in advance). if the test presses don't sound ok, send one of the test press copies to the lacquer cutter, and let the plant know there is a problem. then you have to work it out with both of them as to what needs to be redone, plating or lacquers. this thing does happen from time to time, remember this is not a computerized, digital type of process!

16. at this point you should go ahead and contact the distributors. the distributors are the wholesale buyers of your records. there are distributors who specialize in certain music genres, and some who are more general. you have the best chance of dealing with them if they are small and right for your genre, and if you allow them to make returns to you of any quantity of records that they aren't able to sell. e-mail or call them and try to open an account. be nice to them (at least at first) because they are your buyers. send in your completed account form, and get their shipping address and contact info.

17. make a one page "hype" sheet that describes the record. Include info about the artist, release date, describe the tracks, and be descriptive enough so that it sounds like something people would like to hear. Make three versions of this: one distributor version which includes the price, one store version which does not have the distributor price, and one dj version with space at the bottom for them to give you feedback, rate the record, tell you if they will chart it, etc. charting your record means that they will list it in their top ten playlist either online or in magazines.

18. find some press contacts, i.e. people who review records at magazines. get their mailing addresses.

19. find some dj's who spin the kind of tracks you are putting out, and get their contact information. better yet, join a small dj record pool. a dj record pool is a subscription service that djs pay to join in order to get advance copies of records, and they usually have to qualify with solid credentials. it's generally free for a record label to join, but it means you must send them a certain number of free records that they turn around and send to their dj's.

20. find record stores who sell the kind of tracks you are putting out, especially larger stores in areas far from you.

21. buy record-mailers to ship your white label promo records to all these places once they arrive. the mailers are flat cardboard pieces with indentations in the right spot so you can fold them into boxes that hold one to three records, or you can buy slightly bigger ones that hold more. buying these tends to seem like a waste of money, and there are rumors that some people use free Fedex and UPS packaging material turned inside-out to ship records. this is probably illegal, so it is not recommended. It is also not recommended that you use your kids as Fedex packaging "mules" to help carry large amounts of fedex envelopes and boxes out of the Fedex store.

22. when the white label promos are shipped to you, rejoice and kiss them, do a little happy dance, whatever you need to, because you're almost there and you finally have a bunch of real records. immediately mail the promos to all the contacts on the lists you made. put a hype sheet in with each record and make sure the record is addressed to a person, not just a company. make sure that you reserve some records to bring to local record stores. and when you send them to distributors, send multiple copies, send them to distributors that you haven't even signed up with—they might hear the record and decide they want it.

23. when you bring your record to local stores, they will play it right there in front of you while you try to pretend you're not nervous and act like you don't care what they think. if they like it, they will tell you how many they can take, and you can sell them or exchange them for store credit to buy records at the store. if they don't like it, they will say something along the lines of "i don't think we can really sell this one here." in either case, give them one or two copies for the store, along with a hype sheet. this is just goodwill, and it goes a long way. your local record stores are like your extended family. however, they are not such close family that you want to bring toddlers with you when you try to sell your record there. your kids will quickly realize that the record store equals extreme kid boredom, and this will not only create a negative association with record stores as they grow up, but record stores tend to be small with small aisles and filled with djs trying to buy records (including yours). When a screaming toddler flails on the ground in an act of civil disobedience, it can take its toll on the store's dj clientele.

24. about a week before your release date, start calling or e-mailing the distributors to see if they are going to make an order. if they are, they will give you a quantity and then send an invoice later, or they may just send an invoice.

25. about a day or two before the release date, add up all the distributor orders. this is the amount of records you pre-sold, so it is your best guess at how many records are actually going to sell, because the distributors generally know what is going to sell. not always, but generally. don't get discouraged if the numbers are not as high as you had hoped. it's best to assume that if orders are low, the distributor is just clueless on this one, and if orders are high, then clearly the distributor is absolutely right.

26. make a list of each distributor and the amount of their order, this is called a drop-ship list. send the list to the pressing plant, and they will send the records directly to the distributors in the quantities you specify. the distributor generally pays for shipping from the plant and they will usually ship on a regular basis by combining a bunch of different releases in one weekly shipment.

157

27. make an invoice for each distributor and send it on the date of release.

28. after thirty to sixty days, or whatever terms you agreed to in your distributor contract, send them a reminder that their invoice is due. you may need to send several reminders, make phone calls, leave messages for various people in accounting, send multiple e-mails, etc. . . .

29. once you get your money from the distributors, see if you have cleared a profit or at least broken even.

30. realize you're not in this for the money and go back to step one.

* if house music is not your passion, you can still make a record label!! doesn't matter if it's punk rock or country or some weird glitchy electronica they are really digging in Sweden. you basically just need to change the format, i.e., you might need to make 7" or 10" size records, and find the expert lacquer cutting guys and distributors for your genre.

** very cool secret: you can ask the lacquer mastering guy to put a secret message in on the lacquer when he cuts it, and that message will appear on the inside of the record near the label. just a few words though, (he has to etch it on the lacquer by hand).

SINGING THINGS YOU CAN'T SPEAK

MAIA ROSSINI

An interview with Corin Tucker

This Mama works until her back is sore/but the baby's fed and
the tunes are pure
—*Sleater-Kinney, "Step Aside" from the album* One Beat

SLEATER-KINNEY'S new album *One Beat* was released on August 20, 2002 on the Kill Rock Stars label. For those of you who have not heard it, do yourselves a favor and go buy it. Not only is it one of the first important musical works to react to September 11, but it also chronicles the premature birth of lead singer Corin Tucker's son, and her subsequent journey into motherhood. And Mamas, listen—this album rocks. Hard. Tucker's voice has never sounded so strong and nuanced; the issues that are covered in the songs are incredibly timely and important; and the closing song on the album, "Sympathy," is some of the most gripping music I have ever heard about the power and anguish of mother love. It is an album every Mama ought to have.

I spoke to Tucker on the phone just before the release of the album.

MAIA ROSSINI: The first thing I wanted to ask is, since you're a rock star and a mother, what brand of diapers do you feel keeps your baby dryer than dry?

CORIN TUCKER: (*laughs*) I'm so bad. I totally will only use Pampers. I have a pampered son. I just, you know, I was not going to go for the cloth diapers.

MR: Okay, that's not a real question. Really. Let's start. I'm surprised that more of the world's art isn't made by new mothers. I mean, I know we're all tired, but it's an earth-shaking experience, and it seems that, like romantic love, it should inspire countless songs and paintings and poems, but really, I am tears-in-my-eyes grateful when I hear *Sympathy* or something like Lauryn Hill's *Zion* or even something as mediocre as Madonna's *Butterfly*, because I'm just so happy to hear an artist who's actually expressing the power of motherhood. It's a really rare thing. So, why do you think there isn't more great art written by and about mothers?

CT: I think that it's really true that it's extremely hard to keep your art going when you have to take care of this fragile being. It was really hard for me to keep the band going. Fortunately I have band members that would come to my house, and Carrie and I would just write here. And I'm lucky enough to have a nanny for part of the time. I just don't think that most women have those kind of luxuries. Most women are just keepin' it together when they have a kid. It takes so much work. I wish that our society was more helpful to the moms, because I think it's pretty helpful to the babies, but I think that our society as a whole should be more in tune to how hard it is for a new mother.

MR: Or at least more respectful of it.

CT: Yeah. And more dads should be taking on the childcare.

MR: Well, yeah. I read an article in *Seattle Weekly* about you pretty recently, and I think there was quotation in it where the author was talking about your new album, and how the band was really taking off and everything, and then he wrote, "For all of 2001 she [Corin] did little but nurse and care for her newborn." And then he sort of goes into this list of all the professional accomplishments of your bandmates—what they did during this time, and I kind of winced because that is a monumental, Herculean effort—to take care of a newborn for a year! And I wondered how that year was for you?

CT: You know, it was really hard. It was super hard because my son, Marshall, was born nine weeks early. He was a preemie, and he was in the hospital for two weeks. And he is perfectly healthy and we're extremely fortunate, but it was really scary at first, and the whole thing was really traumatic for me, which is basically where *Sympathy* came from. So, when he came home, he was still under five pounds, just this tiny fragile little guy, and also at the time, my husband had to go shoot a movie. He was basically gone for three months. He came home on the weekends, but I was home alone with this fragile little being, and I kind of went out of my mind. Thankfully I have really great friends and family.

MR: A good support network.

159

CT: Yeah, so that was really great. And you know, you just have to go through it, and fortunately Marshall is super healthy—he's a feisty little guy. It was really good. But it was a hard, hard time for sure.

MR: Aside from being a mother, did you get any work done that year?

CT: Yeah, yeah, I did. That's when we wrote. We started writing when Marshall was five months old, and we wrote a lot. We wrote all during the fall, and all the songs about September 11. We were writing during that whole time.

MR: And I know that there's a lot of creative process between you and your bandmates. Did it change at all? Was it difficult for them to adjust to your motherhood? I sometimes found that with the friends I had before I had a kid, there was a whole new aspect to it afterwards if they didn't have kids. There was a lot of readjustment that needed to happen.

CT: Yeah, I think that I'm just lucky enough that Carrie is such a supportive writing partner that she would just come to my house every day. She moved to Portland. She lived in Olympia and she moved to Portland, and she would just come to my house every day and I would get a babysitter and we would just go in the basement and write, and that's how we wrote this record. We took a lot of stuff to Janet and we did some writing at Janet's house as well, but a lot of this stuff just happened in my basement, because Carrie would just come here, because she knew that there was no other way it was going to happen. I was really lucky.

MR: It was perfect, right? Because you not only get to do your work, but you get that break in the day that every new mother needs

CT: Exactly!

MR: Someone to come over and talk to you and break the boredom for a while.

CT: Totally. The whole thing is that your identity is totally different now. And that was a lot harder than I thought it was going to be. I was just feeling like I wasn't a writer anymore. I was really scared that I wasn't going to be able to do the band anymore, and so I worked as hard as I could on the record, but definitely, my bandmates totally took up the slack.

MR: We go into our pregnancies thinking about these little feet and clever hats, and we come out the other side as totally different people and artists. Was that your experience? Have you experienced a shift in perception?

CT: I think to some degree I feel a changed person by the experience. I just don't take anything for granted. I try not to take anything for granted anymore because just having Marshall here and having everyone be healthy is this really great gift. And I also think that it's made me a more open person to the world. I've always been a really reserved and shy person, and I think that's really easy to foster when you're in a rock band. To not really go out in the world and put yourself out there for people to know you—to care about the world instead of just caring about your own small circle . . .

MR: A teacher I once had, a pretty successful writer and the mother of two boys, was once asked how having kids changed her work. And she said that she became a better writer because time suddenly became more precious, and also that she felt like she had this audience that she didn't want to let down—that she had this personal audience in her son—and that she wanted to be a good writer for her kids and to make them proud. Do you find yourself thinking along those lines? Like when you write your songs, do you find yourself thinking, "What will my son think of this in the future?" and, conversely, are you any less reckless about what you might say or write or put out there?

CT: No. I mean, I think about it after I've written it, and it does cross my mind, and I think, "Well, I hope he'll understand." I think if I let those thoughts get to me then I would censor myself, and that I probably wouldn't have written *Sympathy* because it's such a scary song. I find that I really enjoy being a selfish writer. I write more for myself. And I really wanted to convey the sort of darkness of this song without taking away the sort of scariness of it. That's one of the great luxuries of being in a rock band—it's such a selfish moment—and I treasure it.

MR: And you think you're going to be able to continue that as he gets older and more aware of who you are and what you're putting out there?

CT: I have wondered about that. I have wondered if he'll totally rebel against myself and my husband and become a stockbroker. But he's totally wild. He's loves music and he loves Sleater-Kinney. He was a really big part of when we recorded this record. He was in the studio every day. He learned to walk in the studio. And he loves "One Beat" and he learned to dance to it, you know, he knows how to dance. And he was at our show the other week, and he was freaking-out because he got to play Janet's drums. He's totally wild. So I think his personality is well suited for our lifestyle.

MR: Louise Erdrich once wrote that every mother who is a writer keeps a running list of mother/writers in her head for comfort and solace. Do you have a similar one for mother/musicians and mother/writers?

CT: Oh yeah. Like, one person who has been really kind to me is Kim Gordon. I was actually pregnant and on tour and at her house. And Julie Cafritz as well. They're both moms and in that band, Free Kittens, together, and they were just super supportive and super kind to me. It's just really important to have other people that you know that are still making art and doing stuff, and Kim is definitely one of them. And Kristen Hersh. I know she has, like, three kids and a dog and a husband. They tour in an RV and stuff. There are other moms out there. Actually, one story I have to tell is that when I was pregnant and on tour, we were in Boston and I was hanging out with my friend and I had just told her I was pregnant and she had brought this woman backstage, and we had all bought the new Madonna record and we would listen to it in the car. We were talking about it, and I was obsessing about Madonna on stage and asking people what they thought of her. And so backstage there was this woman and she said, "You know, I think that record really sucks and these women, these artists, after they have babies, their music really goes downhill! I mean, look at Chrissie Hynde!" And she was going off, and Carrie and I just looked at each other and said, "That's not true! What about Kim Gordon? What about Patti Smith?" And we got in this big argument, and you know, I didn't say to this woman that I didn't know that I was pregnant. But it was this weird thing. I don't know if people have that attitude or not, but this woman certainly did.

MR: A lot of people think you get to be either a mother or an artist.

CT: Exactly.

MR: Does Marshall have a favorite song?

CT: He really likes *One Beat*, I think. When we were mixing that I remember he was dancing.

MR: And do you sing him lullabies at night?

CT: I do!

MR: Excellent. And do you sing him songs from the band?

CT: (*laughs*) No, no—I found those songs to not be calming at all. I sing him *Silent Night* and that song about all the pretty horses. That's a really good one.

MR: So, I'm assuming that you've been doing a lot of press to promote this record, and I wondered if your motherhood is seen as a story. Are you asked about it a lot, or is it something that is kind of avoided or shunted aside as a nonstory?

CT: I think that people ask me about it a lot less than I thought they were going to. And connect the song *Sympathy* a lot less than I thought they were going to.

MR: Really?

CT: Yeah, and it's interesting that it's been a lot of male writers. I can't remember which review I just read where they connected that song with romantic love. Even though the words were so bizarrely . . . I mean, I just thought that song was really weird. I didn't think that people were going to like it, because I thought it was this really specific catharsis of this particular thing that happened to me.

MR: But any mother is going to get it. The song made me cry the first time I heard it. Any mother is going to listen to it and connect.

CT: Yeah, and I thought that was who would connect to it—but all these writer guys . . . which is great, I'm glad that people can relate to it. But I was expecting to talk more about Marshall's birth. That's why I requested the *Hip Mama* interview, because I wanted to relate that part of it.

MR: So, one of the main conversations I have over and over with my friends who are both artists and mothers is, how do you find the time? How do you give enough to your baby and your work and not feel kind of shitty about one or the other?

CT: I don't know. (*laughs*) I really don't know. I think that it's just a really intense juggling and balancing act. I've been lucky enough to find a really great nanny. She's really great. But I did feel really guilty when we made our record because I was working. And I was just working forty or fifty hours a week. And that's just what some moms have to do. For me, there was this realization that we have to make a living. It's not like my husband is a super-wealthy artist. We're both sort of struggling artists. We both have to do what we have to do to do our work. And besides the financial part of it, it's also really important to me to be a happy person, just to be doing work that I enjoy. I think that a depressed mom is not a great thing for a kid. They've really found that out in studies and stuff, too. So, I think it's important to take care of myself and keep doing work. But I do feel really guilty about having to go on tour without him.

MR: How old is he now?

CT: He's seventeen months.

MR: Do you remember the first time you kind of stepped away and left him with someone else? Do you remember that moment really clearly?

CT: Oh yeah. It was last December; we played in Seattle. I went up to Seattle with the band. We stayed overnight, and he stayed here with his dad and I called about every five minutes, "He okay? What's he doing?"

MR: He probably did better than you did, right?

CT: Yeah! And every time I do go away, it's like he's fine, and he and his dad get to bond and it's actually a good thing. I come home and the house is clean and I'm like, "Oh my God!"

MR: I should go away more often!

CT: Exactly. And that's a really great thing, to feel that.

163

MR: So your husband is really supportive as far as all this goes, obviously.

CT: Yeah, he is.

MR: Which is key, I'm sure.

CT: So key, so crucial. I thought so much about being a single mom because he was gone so much when I first had Marshall and I was like, "Oh my god, how would you do it alone?" Not just the physical, exhausting labor, but also the emotional feeling of this is so hard. It made me feel like it would be a really hard thing.

MR: And as a last question, I wanted to ask you about your voice. Your amazing, power-ful, critically acclaimed voice. Did you have a definitive moment when you knew you could sing? When you realized that your voice is the instrument that it is?

CT: I've always loved to sing, and sang at home growing up a lot. But I had to battle with my self-esteem to actually think I could be a singer. Riot grrrl really helped me with a lot of those issues, and I started my first band, Heavens to Betsy, with the support of the Olympia community. Our first show was at the Capitol Theater on *Girl Night*, in front of one hundred people, and something intense and magical happened, I think. It's like I could sing things I couldn't speak. People felt this, and told me so.

TALKING BACK TO MY ELDERS

MUFFY BOLDING

> There is no more sombre enemy of good art than the pram in the hall.
> —*Cyril Connolly, literary critic and The Viceroy of Fop*

EVER SINCE the first day that I became a mother, I have railed, with all my might, against Mr. Cyril Connolly's grand pronouncement that along with the creation of life necessarily comes artistic death. And this battle to remain true to myself began long before I had ever even heard of Cyrill Connolly or his definitive edict regarding the output of a uterus in relation to the output of a passionate, determined, albeit stretch-marked and saggy-titted, artist.

Fuck Cyrill Connolly. What did he know, anyway? He was just an embittered, old British queen who preened about like a dandy and fancied himself both the first and last word on all things literary. And despite knocking out a slew of devastatingly witty reviews, he obviously had neither the heart, nor the brain that informs it (nor the muff to intuit it), to even begin to comprehend in what ways a female artist is changed by the presence of that now infamous pram in the hall.

I can say, with complete and utter conviction, that becoming a mother is what made me the artist I am today.

True, it is certainly a much more complicated and difficult path to choose as a writer, fraught with all sorts of untidy pitfalls, like head lice and hemorrhoids, but it does offer a singularly unique outlook on life that simply cannot be supplied by all those filthy, unwashed, Marlboro-bumming, Ginsberg-spouting, coffeehouse-loitering, oh-so-bohemian trolls you were hanging out with in college.

Having a baby provided me with an entirely new set of eyes, ears, and, unfortunately, breasts. It turned me into that most fierce, devoted, and visceral of creatures—a mother. It forced me to see and feel the despair and suffering of others from an entirely different construct. It allowed me to take notice of the aching grace and overwhelming beauty in the seemingly most inconsequential of life's moments.

But, most of all, it made me learn to phone in Chinese take-out, fold laundry, nurse a baby, patiently cater to imaginary friends who wanted their tuna sandwiches cut on the bias instead of straight across, help with fourth grade math that was far and above my intellectual ken, gingerly ward off the advances of an inconveniently libidinous husband, mediate savage Barbie brawls and sibling fisticuffs whilst typing up brilliantly executed prose—all at the same goddamned time.

If it had been the 1970s, I certainly would've qualified as the poster-girl for Valium. But it was the early 90s, and I was on my own. Me, my keyboard, my leaky tits, my engraved, Tiffany silver-plated lice comb, and the mantra that miraculously got me through each day:

I'm typing as fast as I can.

> It was tough trying to keep writing while bringing up three kids, but my husband was totally in it with me, and so it worked out fine. Le Guins' Rule: One person cannot do two fulltime jobs, but two persons can do three fulltime jobs—if they honestly share the work. The idea that you need an ivory tower to write in, that if you have babies you can't have books, that artists are somehow exempt from the dirty work of life—rubbish.
>
> *Ursula K. Le Guin, writer*

Yeah, you ain't kiddin', Le Guin, because when you have children in the house, there is no ivory tower or room of one's own in which to solemnly ponder the human condition, much less write about it. Unless, of course, you count taking a dump all by yourself, which in my particular household is a luxury that is far too much to ask.

During the early years, the only human condition with which you are familiar on a regular basis is the condition of handling other people's feces. That and constantly shoveling or nippling in what caused the download in the first place.

But you do find time, or make it, or simply just take it, because the only other choice is to go mad from the monotony.

> More than in any other human relationship, overwhelmingly more, motherhood means being instantly interruptible, responsive, responsible.
>
> *Tillie Olsen, writer*

Well, Miss Tillie, that's all good and fine and romantic, doll, but it also means the following:

166

Having to give an important interview to a journalist and appear witty, pithy, and totally cool, while locked in your bedroom closet because there are wailing babies and screaming toddlers savagely beating away at your door, your heart, and the already precariously teetering image you have of yourself as a way happenin' hipster. With every bloodcurdling screech in the background, your hipster quotient drops ten painful points. In just fifteen short minutes, you have gone from Janeane Garofalo to Erma Bombeck. The jig is up, baby.

Sitting hunched over your keyboard, frantically banging out a piece that is already a week past deadline—about which cocktails hip Manhattanites are currently imbibing (as if a Fresno housewife would know in the first place)—while serving up a tasty cocktail of your very own to the squirming baby lying on your lap, suckling at your oh, so droopy left spigot.

167

Being forced to carry in one's purse, at all times—as purely as a means of maternal survival—a regular ol' wooden spoon, found in any regular ol' kitchen in America. Only this particular wooden spoon has The Enforcer etched on the handle with a black Sharpie pen, and can be unsheathed and wielded like Excalibur at a moment's notice. Hear me now, and thank me later: I have used it rarely, but drawn it aplenty. The best part of dishing out "spoon justice" is that revealing just the tip of the handle out the top of your purse, "showing wood," as I call it, does the trick more often than not. No decent, self-respecting Italian mother would ever be caught dead without one. Don't believe I really carry it around in my purse? The next time we run into each other at the food co-op, or a parole hearing, remind me to show it to you. I got no shame.

Being completely riveted by ridiculous medical journal articles like the one I read in the waiting room of my doctor's office that said a good OB/Gyn can tell whether or not a woman has had a baby by just one quick glance at her cervix at the far end of his speculum. The following explains how:

The opening of the cervix on a woman who has had enough sense to keep an aspirin clenched tightly between her knees at all times—and who thusly has not borne any children—looks rather like a dimple in the middle of a bagel. Flavor unspecified.

But the cervical opening of a woman who has brought forth life—via her ho-ho, of course—looks remarkably, undoubtedly, and exactly . . . like a smile.

Sentimental people keep insisting that women go on to have a third baby because they love babies, and cynical people seem to maintain that a woman with two healthy, active children around the house will do anything for ten quiet days in the hospital; my own position is somewhere between the two, but I acknowledge that it leans toward the latter.
      Shirley Jackson, writer

Christ, I am so with you on this one, Shirl—you have no idea.

I remember those precious post-delivery days on the maternity wing as some of the most tranquil and heavenly I have ever known. Reading, watching t.v., doing the *New York Times* crossword puzzle in ink (okay, so that's a brazen lie), drowsing, uninterrupted except for the steady stream of delivery dudes stopping by to drop off all the lovely goodies with my name on the card. There is nothing on earth more soothing to a new mother's soul than being waited on, catered to, fussed over, and even babied. And, further, there is nothing on earth more soothing to a new mother's scorching hemmies than a really good sitz bath, but I digress.

Those halcyon hospital days were fleeting—as was the largesse of our HMO—and soon it was back to the regular daily grind, plus, of course, another darling, squalling, sweet-milky-breathed, brand-new mouth to feed.

168

And so, when my children were still very small, I took it upon myself to find many varied and ingenious ways to buy precious time in which to write. I even went against all previous self-righteously held beliefs and purchased a playpen, which, because of my original distaste for that which it signified, I quickly renamed The Oubliette. I derived this oh, so clever sobriquet from the French noun *oubliere*, meaning: a place of forgetting.

And, oh, how I meant to forget.

I would vanquish to the Oubliette whomever was still small, squirmy, and be-diapered enough to fit inside, and place the whole contraption within glancing range of both myself and Mr. Rogers. It was a perfect set-up. Fred would entertain the little beastie with his wonderfully soothing voice, and enlightening visits to crayon factories and the Land of Make Believe, and I could get on with the bidness of etching prose onto page or slammin' words to pixel, depending on whether you still hold romantic notions about the job of writing.

I do not.

> By and large, mothers and housewives are the only workers who do not have regular time off. They are the great vacationless class.
> *Anne Morrow Lindbergh, writer*

Now, that is so what I'm talkin' about, Anne.

Mothers get very few vacations from their jobs, and even when they do manage to find a weekend here or there, their real work—their children—are never far from their minds.

For the most part, the only real childfree vacations I have known since becoming a mother are working vacations. That is, vacations that are taken to either further one's career aspirations or to quickly refill one's coffers because the power is about to be shut-off for nonpayment.

However, being fortunate enough to do what I do for a living, I can hardly complain. My regular trips to Los Angeles and points beyond, to work with producers, directors, and editors, as well as other writers and actors, have afforded me the unique opportunity to meet many remarkable people—people that most working moms could only dream of shooting the shit with. Trust me, this little working-class Sicilian dame knows very well how favored her life has been, and not a day goes by that I don't light a candle and say a novena of thanks to the Baby Jesus.

I have found myself in the goddamndest of places, sitting across from the goddamndest of people. Sometimes, I even pinch myself under the table, just to make sure I'm not dreaming, and sometimes I do it just to punish myself for being so fucking lucky. And then sometimes I just do it because, when done in the right place and with just the right amount of pressure, that shit can turn a girl on . . . but of this, I shall speak no more.

One of the most meaningful of those occasions found me lounging in the swanky Four Seasons Hotel, drinking iced tea and talking to Rosanna Arquette about what it means to be a woman and a mother, working in Hollywood today. We spoke of her documentary, *Searching for Debra Winger*, in which she seeks to understand the reasons why female artists are cast-aside the minute they sprout grey hair or a wrinkle. She does this through a series of provocative and revealing interviews with other actresses who have felt the same sting of age discrimination that she herself has known—strong, talented women like Frances McDormand, Ally Sheedy, Tracy Ullman, Whoopi Goldberg, and Debra Winger herself, among many others. I told Rosanna that with this feisty, formidable lot fighting the good fight for us all, I felt both in safe hands and in good company.

Looking both lovely and luminous— and using a voice filled with passion and righteous indignation—she told me, "Just when we're getting good and ripe and interesting, just when we're finding our true selves and becoming comfortable with that self we find, just when we have the most wisdom and insight to share with others, we are cast aside for a younger, perkier model with a higher 'fuckability factor.' That's show-biz."

In making this critically acclaimed documentary, she hopes to help change the societal perception that once a woman becomes a mother, or reaches "a certain age," she can no longer be sexy as a woman or vital as an artist. This most courageous and heartfelt undertaking, as I understood it, was conceived and created to benefit all female artists, not the least of whom is her young daughter, Zoe.

I came away from my time with Rosanna completely beguiled and inspired, as a woman and as an artist, and especially as a mother. I remain changed by her words and charged by her commitment to kickin' ass and takin' names in the world of art.

Another amazing occurrence, that would not otherwise have been visited upon the life of my humble little family were it not for my work as a writer and actor, was a recent Fourth of July shin-dig in Los Angeles that I attended with my husband and 9-year-old son. Present at this casual get-together were many good friends and colleagues with whom I have had both the pleasure and privilege of working. Among these, one stands out for the extraordinary friendship that we forged on a film set in far-off Romania.

You know him as Francis, the spoiled little bastard who heisted Pee Wee Herman's bike in the film, Pee Wee's Big Adventure. I know him as Markie Holton, great friend and actor extraordinaire. When he first showed up, he had the audacity to introduce himself to me, as if I didn't already know his work and who he was. As if.

So, while we wiled away the hours awaiting our calls to set, he and I shared cigarettes, gossip, extraneous ham products (the Romanians love their ham products), and stories of our families back home. I told him that my son, Hunter, was the world's biggest

169

Pee Wee fan, and that he was going to die when he found out who I had been hanging with during my oft-bemoaned, month-long absence from him and his sisters.

When the shoot was finally over, we hugged and kissed and vowed to keep in touch, and then returned home to the world of mortals and mortgages. Months passed until we found ourselves together once again on Independence Day. Obviously Markie remembered what I had told him about Hunter, and with that in mind, he did the most remarkable thing. He led Hunter and I into a quiet room, closed the door, and proceeded to give a one-on-one, condensed command performance of Francis, just for my son.

"Today's my birthday, and my father said I can have anything I want. So guess what I want. I want your bike, Pee Wee!"

My son just stood there, blinking and smiling. He couldn't have beamed anymore if he'd been standing directly on home plate at Comiskey Field during a night game double-header, if there even is such a thing. He just looked up at Mark and said, "Thank you, Mr. Holton." Mark, in all his gracious glory, replied, "No, Hunter, thank you. You just made my year, son."

Oh, and Markie? You made mine.

> Having a family is like having a bowling alley installed in your brain.
> *Martin Mull, actor*

Yeah, yeah, yeah—I know Martin Mull isn't a mother, and hasn't the vagina to even try and fake it 'til he makes it. I just loved the absolute clanging, crashing, crushing truth of this quote.

> Motherhood means mental freeze . . .
> *Kim Deal, The Breeders, No Aloha*

Kim, honey, I beg you to set down the draft beer, the Marlboro, and that purely genius guitar of yours, and to please remember that what I am about to say comes from the heart and from the mouth of someone who has actually worn a hand-scrawled DIY t-shirt that says, "I Wanna Be Kim Deal," as well as someone who staunchly lists you as part of the unquestionable, untouchable Unholy Triumvirate of Music Deities. So, please remember to keep that in mind when I say what I am about to say:

Fuck you.

Yes, you probably have loads more fun than I do, getting drunk every night, touring across the country unfettered by any familial or domestic obligations, writing and performing extraordinary music, much of which has provided a quite apt and potent soundtrack for more years of my life than I'd care to accurately tally.

You get to smoke dope and shoot pool all night long, without ever having to worry about being woken up at 5:00 A.M. by someone who wants you to sing the Charlie Brown "dun dun dun dun dun dun dun dun . . . dun dun dun" theme song to them one more time, because they "can't memember it."

You get to work wherever you want to or whenever you feel like it—whenever the muse, or the Jack Daniels, hits you just right. You don't have to wait for a cranky, drowsy toddler to nod off, or for a 16-year-old to finally fall asleep, after sitting with her and holding her and listening to her cry for hours over some boy or other; weeping as if her heart is breaking, because it is.

You get to fuck whomever you want, whenever you want, with no worries that some short person is going to wander into the room whilst you are in flagrante delicto, thereby forcing you to use your brilliant creativity, not for the betterment of your art, but for quickly and cleverly coming up with the lie that you and Daddy "are planning a very special family trip to Disneyland right now, so could you please go back into the living room and watch the *Little Mermaid* so we can get all the plans just right?"

And you certainly don't have to worry about socking away enough money to cover the cost of extensive psychotherapy for that child—the need for which will undoubtedly surface in about twenty-five years, thanks to the unthinkable horror and searing trauma that the previously mentioned incident will most likely leave on his or her tender psyche.

You don't have a lot of the same worries, obstacles, hassles, and headaches as an artist that I do, Kim Deal. But, I assure you, I possess many things that you do not.

Aside from all the obvious stuff—stuff about which I am sure you could give a shit anyway, like the birthday parties, the first day of school, the first time you hear them say "mama," the first time they drag toilet paper through actual crack instead of just over cheek—there is the added insight into the work, into the very words themselves.

Just as nature intended it to, motherhood has heightened all of my senses, and that can't help but bleed over into my work as an artist. My entire view of the world has changed, especially as it relates to my work. I now see much deeper into the process of writing itself—into the stories, the motivations, and especially the characters as they relate to one another.

You see, Kim, when you sober up enough to watch a Disney movie (okay, so you'd never watch a fucking Disney movie, much less sober up specifically enough to do so, but I'm on a roll here, so work with me, okay?) you will forever be the Princess.

You get to watch *Cinderella, Sleeping Beauty, Snow White*, and the *Little Mermaid*, and endlessly recapture what it felt like to be her, waiting for her prince to come, just like he inevitably always does in fairy tales. You will always see the world through the eyes, albeit blurry and bloodshot, of the Princess.

When I watch those movies now, my eyes gaze at the prince, not with hope and lust and longing, but with the steely, perceptive eye of a guardian, a chaperone, a parent, a protector. I am sizing him up, not to see if I wish to ride off with him into the sunset on a white horse, but to see if he's good enough to provide my princess with the happily-ever-after she so richly deserves (and I so fervently demand.)

I do this, not because I have lost the ability to see the world through the starry eyes of a young maiden—the memories of that fine and ripe time of my life will never leave me—but because I have experienced a profound metamorphosis.

I am now the benevolent fairy godmother, the kindly dwarf, and the stern sea king with a really sharp trident who will bust a pitchfork in your ass if you don't treat my little girl like the princess that she be.

In other words, as an artist, I get to cross over into an entirely different way of seeing the world around me, and thusly an entirely different way of processing it through my work. I get to climb up on the refrigerator, legs dangling, and see the kitchen in a way I never could have before. I get to become a whole new person, and a whole new artist.

But, you see, Kim, I fully realize that mine is ultimately a more difficult and complicated path to choose as an artist— but also ultimately so much more rewarding. My work would not be nearly as hopeful or open or bound to humanity—both my own and the world's—were it not informed by my experience as a mother. Having children has made me a writer in a way that I was not before, as now, everything matters.

I can no longer simply sit back, wearing black, yawning, smoking Gitanes cigarettes, espousing bored nihilism, and mocking the earnest attempts of others to make better this world we live in; I have children.

I now have a very real stake in how this grand and glorious story unfolds and reveals itself; I have children.

172

I now care passionately about this world and the future and how it all turns out; I have children.

And a cervix that smiles.

AFTERWORD

BEE LAVENDER

SEVERAL YEARS ago I took my family to the first Ladyfest in Olympia, Washington. The center of the tiny town was swarming with people, mostly young women wearing the uniform of urban hipster, Northwest style—bobbed hair and vintage clothes mixed with handmade accessories. Someone was reading a *Time* magazine and I looked over her shoulder. Olympia had just been written up as the "hippest town in America" with a picture of the band Sleater-Kinney.

I was in town for the festival, to do a workshop about radical parenting, and my nine-year-old daughter had volunteered to sing on the main stage with a folk protest chorus. She looked wan. Her freckles stood out against the pallor of her face, and she had dark circles under her eyes. "I'm nervous," she said, and tears started to trickle from her eyes.

The chorus members, all over the age of twenty and a few in their thirties, gathered around. Someone patted her on the back. "It's okay, Mina," one of the women said, "you don't have to sing." Mina shook her head and burst into tears.

"Come on, Sweetie, let's go inside and check out the theatre. Do you remember coming here when you were little, before we moved away?" She shook her head and took my hand and we walked inside.

I attended college in this town, and had a baby at the end of my freshman year. My girl spent her infancy crawling around seminar rooms, climbing library shelves, running and laughing across the square. She grew into a hazel-eyed, rabble-rousing toddler with ratty blonde punk-rock hair she cut herself, pink dresses, duck boots, fearless grace. She was a fleet-footed child, and notoriously prone to stripping naked in the cafeteria, jumping on top of a table, and serenading the astonished lunch crowd. My memories of college largely involve trailing along behind, calling out for her to slow down, to let me catch up.

Mina was still crying about the performance as we walked into the auditorium. I was astonished that she was nervous; she has always been my personal hero when it comes to performing in front of audiences. Where I am shy and bookish, she is brave and sociable. I keep her example firmly in mind when I'm nervous before a reading. I squeezed her hand. She entered the huge, red-carpeted theatre and stopped halfway to the stage. She looked up at the women setting up their equipment for sound check. "You mean," she turned to me, her complexion suddenly rosy and her hazel eyes bright again, "I'm opening for Sleater-Kinney?" She laughed and started jumping up and down, all of her fear gone, ecstatic over the prospect of singing on the same stage as what she called "the coolest band in the world."

We moved away from Olympia after college, and I had another child and a whole new set of adventures. As an infant, my son required silence and a pristine sense of respite, at all times. He did not like crowds and panicked over even insignificant stress, like standing in a school hallway. Larger events caused paralytic pain. As a toddler, he was known to pass out with fright at the prospect of library story-time. He expressed a deep and sincere desire to wear suits and bow ties each day, negotiated advantageous deals with the tooth fairy, and at age five published a zine about Legos.

With one extroverted child and one introverted child, a mathematician husband who traveled frequently, and a career of my own, it wasn't clear to me how I could possibly satisfy all of the competing demands of our family. So I did the only reasonable thing: I sighed, shrugged, and cast aside my own expectations about how people are supposed to live and work. Since I had become a mother at the end of my own adolescence, I didn't have all that many preconceived notions to shed.

I learned that children thrive when their parents are happy; that hanging out with toddlers is more fun than partying; that it is possible and even desirable to be creative and nurturing at the same time; that good work and motherhood are not antithetical, but rather, simply a calling. I decided to accept whatever might come my way. Mothers and children want and deserve art, literature, challenging conversations, complicated friendships, and it is just as important to sustain aesthetic standards as it is to feed the children promptly. By watching my own children and welcoming their lessons, I learned to be more outspoken and daring, but at the same time to stay safe and take care of myself and others.

I befriended artists and musicians and writers and single-parents and other risk-takers. I worked full-time for *Hip Mama* creating and sustaining a massive online community of parents, joined by their mutual need for recognition of their hard work, for entertainment and information. I depended on the couple across the street, a midwife and blues guitarist, for bartered childcare. I joined a radical chorus, paid for extra child care when I had the cash, and when I didn't, packed up the kids and traveled. The Hip

Mama road show put on events and readings up and down both coasts with our own children in attendance, and when our kids were at camp or with friends, we welcomed audiences that included crying babies, laughing toddlers, little boys banging on pianos, girls crawling up the podium and seizing the microphone. My friends helped me, and I helped them, and we were all able to work more and be good parents at the same time.

Not that being a mother, regardless of career choice, is easy. There were times when my children were younger that stand out as the lowest points of misery—pacing the floor with screaming infants, tending to kids with chicken pox or grotesque eye infections, trying to make deadlines when both kids are out of school. Or the exhausting effort of making sure that everyone is safe and happy, that the marriage isn't neglected in favor of the work and children. But there are many examples of successful artistic families, and I made diligent efforts to find those people, to create and maintain community.

We went to the festival in Olympia as a family excursion, with three of us performing and the sensitive child resting with artist friends in a house down the street. We stood in line with the chorus and prepared to walk onstage. Down sets of steps, up others, careful not to trip on cords or stumble against amps. We walked on stage and stood in front of the audience, a thousand or more people packed into the auditorium, crushed up against the stage.

We started to sing. We sang Loretta Lynn and Wanda Jackson; we sang *Bread and Roses*.

Then it was Mina's turn. One of the women covered the microphone with a puppet and a few chorus members leaned over to ask Mina if she wanted to do the song solo or with our help. Mina waved her hand dismissively and pushed the puppet off the microphone.

She started to sing.

As soon as you're born grownups check where you pee
Then they decide just how you're supposed to be
Girls pink and quiet
Boys noisy and blue
It seems like a dumb way to choose what you'll do. . . .

And the crowd went wild, screaming support at the little girl wearing a black velvet cowboy hat, drowning out the chorus of the song.

Now grownups watch closely
Each move that we make
Boys must not cry
And girls must make cake
It's all very formal
and I think it smells

Her voice was fine and high, and the crowd was in an ecstasy of screams. Mina was a rock star, and she ended the song.

175

ABOUT THE CONTRIBUTORS

ABOUT THE EDITORS

BEE LAVENDER is the thirty-three-year-old mother of two children (one a teenager) and the publisher of *Hipmama.com*. She created and publishes *Girl-Mom*, an advocacy site for teen parents. Her work has appeared in numerous anthologies, publications, and radio programs, and her underground zine series *A Beautiful Final Tribute* sold out multiple editions. Her first book was B*reeder: Real Life Stories from the New Generation of Mothers*. Bee is currently working on a memoir about danger and safety. She lives in Cambridge, England, with her family.

MAIA ROSSINI is a writer, editor, and work-at-home mom. She is executive producer at *Mamaphonic.com* and a producer at *Hipmama.com*. She is currently living the writer's life among the wild roses and tumbled rock walls of upstate New York. She lives with her husband Ryan Kelly, and her son Thelonious Spike Kelly-Rossini. She graduated in 1998 from the New School University with an MFA in Creative Writing.

ABOUT THE CONTRIBUTORS

ROSE ADAMS lives Dartmouth, Nova Scotia. Her artwork can be found in collections including the Canada Council Art Bank and Nova Scotia Art Bank. Themes of memorial and the relationship between science and art surface in her artworks, which now include references to motherhood and evolution. Rose teaches in the Foundation department at the Nova Scotia College of Art and Design and is currently the Artist-in-Residence in the Geriatric Clinic at the Queen Elizabeth II Hospital.

EILEEN ALDEN is the co-owner/manager of soulmine records (www.soulmine records.com) a bay area house music record label, and was previously the production manager for imperial dub recordings. eileen is also a member of the punk band the lactators and lives in oakland, with her husband, two sons, dog, and cat.

KATHERINE ARNOLDI has received two New York Foundation of the Arts Awards, the DeJur Award, and the Henfield TransAtlantic Fiction Award. *The Amazing True Story of a Teenage Single Mom* was awarded two American Library Association Awards, and was nominated for the Will Eisner Award in the Graphic Novel.

MONICA BOCK is an associate professor of art at the University of Connecticut, Storrs. She has exhibited widely in such venues as Chicago's Museum of Contemporary Art, Pittsburgh's Mattress Factory, Mobius in Boston, and Art in General in New York City. She received her BA '82 in art from Oberlin College, and spent three years in Japan on a post-bac fellowship from the Oberlin Shansi Memorial Association. She received her BFA '89 and MFA '91 in sculpture from the School of the Art Institute of Chicago, where she became an adjunct assistant professor before accepting her current teaching position in Connecticut in 1996. She has received a variety of awards including an Arts Midwest/NEA Regional Visual Arts Fellowship.

JACEY BOGGS is all over the place. She loves avocados, brightly painted walls, and Blake Schwarzenbach. She used to want to be a writer, but gave that up to be a woodworker. She runs *carveGirl*(.com) where she focuses on original and commissioned functional art. She's also a massage therapist, an anarchist, and a superhero (if you measure by her high hedonic level). She, her rockin' partner, and her spitfire of a son move often, searching for a place that feels like home.

MUFFY BOLDING is a mother/writer/withered debutante who likes the smell of asparagus pee and remains obsessed with the bathroom hygiene of her three children—despite the fact that they are seventeen, thirteen, and ten. She is blissfully married to a cute boy who looks just like Willie Wonka, yet remains tragically in love with the dead poet Ted Hughes. Ms. Bolding lives in Southern California, where she enjoys typing words, making movies, and plucking the rings from the fingers of the dead. She has the mouth of a Teamster and her patron saint is Rocco (pestilence relief). Along with writing for television, film, and various print and online publications, Ms. Bolding publishes the zine *Withered Debutante*. Her work can be found online at www.muffybolding.com.

GAYLE BRANDEIS is the author of *Fruitflesh: Seeds of Inspiration for Women Who Write* (HarperSanFrancisco), *Dictionary Poems* (Pudding House Publications), and *The Book of Dead Birds: A Novel* (HarperCollins), which won Barbara Kingsolver's Bellwether Prize for Fiction in Support of a Literature of Social Change. Her other cool Barbara-centric awards include Barbara Mandigo Kelley Peace Poetry Prize and a grant from the Barbara Deming Memorial Fund for Feminist Artists. Her poetry, fiction, and essays have appeared in dozens of magazines and anthologies, including *Salon.com*, *Nerve*, and *Hip Mama*. Gayle holds a BA in "Poetry and Movement: Arts of Expression, Meditation and Healing" from the University of Redlands, and an MFA in creative writing/fiction from Antioch University. She is on the faculty of the UCLA Writers Program, and is writer in residence for the Mission Inn Foundation's Family Voices Project. She lives in Riverside, California, with her husband and two kids.

ZOFIA BURR is associate professor of English at George Mason University. She is the author of *Of Women, Poetry, and Power: Strategies of Address in the Poetry of Dickinson, Miles, Brooks, Lorde, and Angelou*, and the editor of *Set in Motion: Essays, Interviews, Dialogues*, by A.R. Ammons. Her poetry has most recently appeared in *Delmar*, and in a series of collaborative installations and performances at Mobius in Boston, Artemisia in Chicago, and Soho 20 Chelsea in NYC.

J. ANDERSON COATS is a writer, historian, and librarian, but not necessarily in that order. At twenty-two, she graduated magna cum laude with departmental honors from Bryn Mawr College with a degree in history and a son in preschool. Currently, she lives in New Jersey with her husband, her son, and a cat with thumbs.

KRISTINA JORDAN COBARRUBIA has studied flamenco for close to twenty years, both in the U.S. and in Spain, and performs regularly in San Diego. She's also a writer/producer and will have a short story published in an upcoming issue of *Ladybug* magazine. She lives with her patient husband, two young children, and a pesky cat.

ROSANA CRUZ worked as an organizer and administrator in various organizations for social change in a former life. This work, along with random waitressing jobs, bankrolled more radical grassroots volunteer work and a lot of wanderlust. Currently Rosana balances family life with various writing and music projects and full time pursuit of a master's degree in Latin American studies.

HEATHER CUSHMAN-DOWDEE is the artist/creator of Hathor the Cowgoddess, a cartoon superhero that wants to save the world through a combination of attachment parenting, unschooling, and other rebellious behavior. Hathor appears in gigantic glitter and sharpie pen paintings, tiny sculpey sculptures, mommy-daughter gallery installations, homebirth home video screenings, the random public breastmilk-bread bake-in, and as many cartoons as can be drawn while still giving Heather time for her family. Heather currently lives somewhere in Los Angeles and just gave birth (unassisted!) to her third daughter. Her work can be seen online at www.hathorthecowgoddess.com

DEWI L. FAULKNER is a mamawriterworkerbee living in Van Nuys, California. Her husband, Jonathan, has a great smile and puts up with a lot. Her children, Brooks and Gabrielle, are highly smoochable. Dewi's essays have appeared in *The Banyan Review*, *Hip Mama*, *The Philosophical Mother*, and *Ms. Fitness*. Her writing is also featured online at www.littlemotors.org. Dewi holds a BA in anthropology from UCLA and an MFA in creative writing from Antioch University.

LAURA FOKKENA's writing has appeared in several publications in the U.S. and the Middle East, and in the anthologies *Expat: Women's True Tales of Life Abroad* and *The Contemporary Reader*. She grew up in Iowa but lived for a time in Germany and then in Egypt before earning a master's degree in international development and moving to Boston to co-found a nonprofit organization. She has one daughter, Rakaya.

RACHEL HALL's recent work has appeared or is forthcoming in *The Gettysburg Review*, the *Chicago Tribune*, *Room of One's Own*, and *New Letters*, which awarded her their fiction prize in 2003. She has received other honors and awards from Glimmer Train, Nimrod, Lilith, the Bread Loaf Writers' Conference and the Constance Saltonstall Foundation for the Arts. She teaches creative writing at the State University of New York—Geneseo, where she holds the Chancellor's Award for Excellence in Teaching.

AYUN HALLIDAY is the sole staff member of the quarterly zine, *The East Village Inky*, the 2002 Firecracker Alternative Book Award winner for best zine 2002. She is the author of *The Big Rumpus: A Mother's Tale from the Trenches*, *No Touch Monkey! And Other Travel Lessons Learned Too Late*, and most recently, *Job Hopper: The Checkered Career of a Downmarket Dilettante*. In addition to penning *Bust* magazine's *Mother Superior* column, she contributes to NPR, *Bitch*, and more anthologies than you can shake a stick at without dangling a participle. She lives in Brooklyn with Greg Kotis and their well documented children. She can be found at www.ayunhalliday.com.

LISA MAERAE HINZMAN is a mother, a rocker in the bands MaeRae and NoahJohn, a writer, a mover and shaker, and a self-proclaimed outstanding baker of pies. She lives in Madison, Wisconsin, with her daughter, Ruby, her sweetheart, Matthew, and her two cats, Maeve and Gibson.

MARRIT INGMAN is a freelance writer whose work has appeared in the *Austin Chronicle*, *Isthmus*, *Coast Weekly*, *Alternet*, *Clamor*, and *Mamalicious*. She is a contributing reviewer for the *Chronicle*. Her first book, a memoir of postpartum depression, will be published by Seal Press. She also works as a filmmaker and is currently developing a self-produced documentary on alternative parenting in the United States. She lives in Austin, Texas, with her family.

KATIE KAPUT is a (no longer teenage, but close) transsexual supermom who lives with her two year old son, Rio, and partner, Ricky (a superpapa if ever there was one), in Palo Alto, California. She is working on a novel and dreaming city-kid dreams of moving to Ricky's rural hometown. She grew up in Chicago in a large Italian/Irish family full of noise and love.

PATRICIA KINNEY's work has appeared in *Hip Mama*, *The Sun*, *Stream Ticket*, *Poetry Motel*, *Poetry Magazine.com*, *Ducts*, *Lifeboat*, *Poets Against War*, *Easy Rider*, and various other publications. She birthed and mothers six sons. Kinney received her MFA in creative writing from Antioch University in Los Angeles. She is a full-time writer and plans to teach creative writing workshops in Portland, Oregon, where she recently moved.

VICTORIA LAW is the mother of one feisty little dragon. When not chasing her daughter, she works with incarcerated women, sends books to prisoners, does documentary photography, and writes. Her writing has appeared on-line on *Mamaphonic* and *Banshee Studios* and has been published by *Clamor*, *Austin ABC*, and various zines. Her photos have been published in the *Village Voice*, *Giant Robot*, the *IndyPendent*, and *Clamor*, and have appeared in numerous exhibitions at ABC No Rio, a community arts space in New York City.

SIU LOONG LAW ENGLANDER is a self-proclaimed dragon, champion, and butterfly fairy. She has been taking pictures since she was two and has had her photography published in the zine *Mama Sez No War*. She is currently involved in putting up street art against the RNC.

BETH LUCHT is a mother and writer based in Madison, Wisconsin. An exhausted clinical social worker by day, she fantasizes about quitting the rat race and supporting herself by waiting tables, freelancing, and selling the junk she and her son trashpick on eBay.

LISA PEET lives with her wonderful son and handsome little dog in a house on a hill in the North Bronx. A graduate of New York's School of Visual Arts, she is a baker, illustrator, and writer and works in publishing to keep things interesting.

LORI PFEIFFER hit many mommy milestones on time and journals regularly. She writes long hand because her three-year-old hogs the computer. She authored *The Insiders' Guide to Phoenix* (Globe Pequot, 2001) and writes for *Arizona Highways* and others. She and her spouse Matthias are creating an endless summer for Max in Arizona. She teaches nonfiction writing at Phoenix College.

JUSTYNA SEMPRUCH holds a PhD in comparative literature from the University of British Columbia in Vancouver, Canada. Her research areas are concentrated in feminist theories, family studies, and literature of diaspora and displacement. She is a mother of a five-year-old boy and is currently involved in a postdoc research project on "The Politics of Parenthood and its Impact on Women's Employment" at the University of Basel in Switzerland, as well as in publishing her first book *Tracing Cultural Un/belonging. The Witch in Western Feminist Theory and Literature*.

FIONA THOMSON is a single mom, dyke, and activist living in the San Francisco Bay Area. She works as an editor for a nonprofit publisher, and remembers a time when she used to make elaborate and questionably legal public art.

JENNIFER THORPE promised herself she wasn't going to leave her old life behind when she became pregnant. Consequently, her life is full and rich and she is on the verge of physical collapse and mental exhaustion at all times. She is the singer of Submission Hold; an artist, designer and screenprinter of her own line of kids shirts; works part-time as a mental health worker at the first supervised injection site in North America; and is the proud mother of Sam Danger. Sam continues to rock her world, and she, his.

INGRID WENDT's books of poems include *Moving the House* (BOA); *Singing the Mozart Requiem* (Breitenbush), which received the Oregon Book Award for poetry; and most recently, *Blow the Candle Out* (Pecan Grove Press). She has co-edited *From Here We Speak:*

An Anthology of Oregon Poetry and *In Her Own Image: Women Working in the Arts*, and she is the author of *Starting With the Little Things: A Guide to Writing Poetry in the Classroom*. She has taught for twenty-five years in the Arts-in-Education program in Oregon, Utah, Iowa, and Washington, and has been a Fulbright Professor in Germany. A pianist by training, she lives with her husband, writer Ralph Salisbury, in Eugene, Oregon, where she is a member of the Motet Singers, an a cappella women's ensemble of ten.

LLI WILBURN travels frequently, and relocates occasionally, to places she picks off of a map. After graduating from art school in New York, she embarked on an extended road trip/art project that led her to Oregon, where artistic recognition coincided with unexpected motherhood. Currently she lives with her daughter in Pittsburgh but can often be found elsewhere.

ACKNOWLEDGEMENTS

BEE OFFERS gratitude to her children, Mina and Aubrey, who demonstrated extraordinary patience during the production of this book while simultaneously moving to a new country. She thanks her husband, Byron, and his parents for raising such a nifty kid. Anne Elizabeth Moore is a daring and delightful travel companion and friend. The book would not have been possible without the love and support of Laina Lavender, the most courageous and hardworking and hilarious mother a person could hope to meet.

Maia wishes to thank all four of her parents, Mom, Dad, Lynn and Zak, for providing such great examples on how to balance loving parenting, artistic vision, and their own precious sanity. She wishes to thank Chris, Mary, Tim, Achille, Gina, Max, Ren, and Annie-Roes for all sibling related help and love. Also Tom and Ev, Tom and Kathy, Marilyn and Wally, and Susan and Kurtis for their support and encouragement. And biggest love and gratitude of all goes to her son Spike and husband Ryan for their inspiration, patience, grilled cheese sandwiches, and love.

The editors applaud Susan Presley, resident *Mamaphonic* librarian, for rigorous attention to the details that make heady ideas into real projects. They also send good wishes to Richard Eion Nash and everyone at Soft Skull Press, who do hard work with wit and humor.

Stella Marrs designed the cover of this book. Through her work, her life, her family, and her friendship she sets an impeccable standard and leads by example.

There were hundreds of good submissions that could not fit in this book, and the editors thank every single person who shared a story.

Above all, the editors offer tribute to the community of mothers and artists at *Mamaphonic.com*.